SUNNYLANDS
America's Midcentury Masterpiece
Janice Lyle

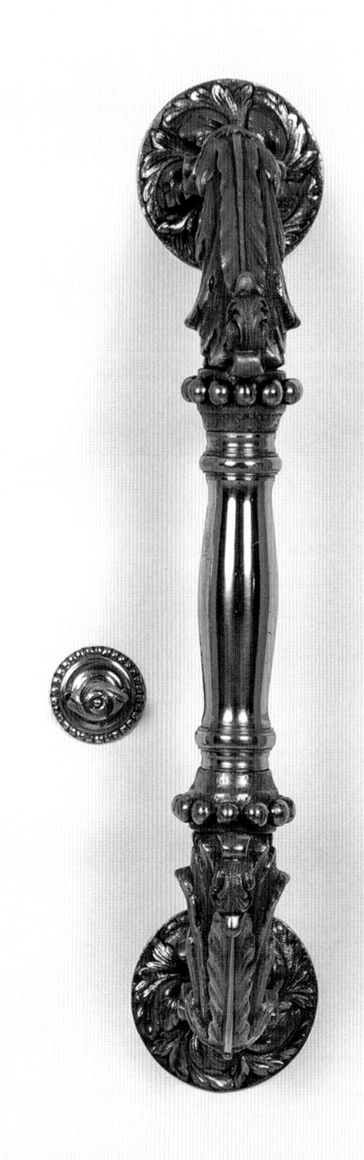

SUNNYLANDS

America's Midcentury Masterpiece

Text by JANICE LYLE
Foreword by MICHAEL S. SMITH
Principal Photography by MARK DAVIDSON

A Stephen Drucker Book
THE VENDOME PRESS
NEW YORK

CONTENTS

FOREWORD

MAGIC FROM SAND

Looking out across the vast Coachella Valley from my house in Rancho Mirage, I see a glorious patchwork of houses, palm trees, swimming pools, and golfers moving back and forth over the lush fairways and greens. In the background, near the foot of the San Jacinto Mountains, a wide swath of mature trees and foliage rises from the desert floor like a fairytale oasis. In the near distance, I can also discern the signature pink walls and stepped roof of Sunnylands, the celebrated desert estate of Ambassador Walter Annenberg and his wife, Leonore.

The true scale of Sunnylands' two hundred verdant, water-fed acres is thrown into high relief by the stark, white, flat desert that surrounds the estate, much of it part of the roughly nine hundred acres assembled by Walter Annenberg while building the sprawling compound and in subsequent years. Conjuring such an oasis out of desert sand in 1963 was no mean feat. In retrospect, the idea of building a private golf course, vast gardens, and a house that would begin quite simply but ultimately grow to 29,000 square feet seems unbelievably daunting. But like all visionary American country house builders, the Annenbergs were creating a home that would evolve to accommodate the expansive life they imagined for themselves and their esteemed guests.

The list of monumental estates constructed by true American visionaries includes John D. Rockefeller's Kykuit in Westchester County, New York; Cornelius Vanderbilt II's the Breakers in Newport, Rhode Island; tractor heir John Deering's Vizcaya in Miami, Florida; and perhaps the closest antecedent of Sunnylands, San Simeon, the insanely ambitious passion project of another publishing magnate, William Randolph Hearst. San Simeon so captivated the public's attention that it was a central character in director Orson Welles's thinly veiled cinematic depiction of Hearst, *Citizen Kane*. The opening credits of the film famously begin with a newsreel view of the fictional estate, Xanadu, accompanied by a quote from a Samuel Taylor Coleridge poem: "In Xanadu did Kubla Khan/A stately pleasure-dome decree."

The idea of building a fertile retreat where there was once only desert attracted the Annenbergs for many reasons. It was a place to play golf, an activity they both loved, as well as a refuge from cold East Coast winters. But it was also a self-contained pleasure dome that would become a seat of social and political power for almost four decades, visited by celebrities of stage and screen, Supreme Court justices, and—during the Annenbergs' lifetime—seven U.S. presidents.

The Annenbergs assembled an amazing design team for the project. Their decision to engage movie star-turned-decorator William "Billy" Haines to work alongside the widely respected California architect A. Quincy Jones was incredibly prescient. Both designers grasped the Annenbergs' desire for a fresh paradigm of American glamour, a modernist country house sensitive to both the region and the climate, but also an impressive background for their extraordinary collection of Impressionist paintings. The breathtaking main house at Sunnylands, centered on Rodin's seductive, patinated-bronze sculpture *Eve*, sets the heroic tone for guests and visitors. For William Haines, the interiors represented a tricky balancing act: the need to accommodate the Annenbergs' diverse collections, which encompassed fantastic Chinese porcelain and incredible china, crystal, and silver; the requirements of entertaining on a grand scale, which the Annenbergs would hone during their years in London at the American ambassador's residence at Winfield House in Regent's Park;

Pages 12–13 Circles and squares: The entry court, with its radial lines, is a contrast to the boxy geometry of the cantilevered entrance.

Below It is hard to grasp that the expansive architecture and park-like setting were entirely man-made from two hundred acres of blow sand and creosote bushes.

and, not least of all, the couple's very specific tastes and sensibility.

What comes across is a highly original but cohesive aesthetic that demonstrates the influence of other designers and furniture makers of the times, including Samuel Marx, T.H. Robsjohn-Gibbings, and even the Paris workshops of Maison Jansen. The interiors are both elegant and cinematic and infused with an unexpected dash of humor and wit, exemplified by the large sunflower print fabric in the Game Room, the tortoise-patterned leather on the dining room's Regency-inspired chairs, and the celadon-on-celadon trapunto quilting on much of the seating.

This icon of American country house building, with its flower-filled guest rooms and glamorous public spaces, reflects an enduring Palm Springs style—not the clichéd assemblage of cold, midcentury modern furniture and objects, but a refined, worldly aesthetic that reflects a kaleidoscope of extraordinary interests and experiences. It's almost impossible to imagine what it was like to be a guest at Sunnylands in its heyday: the procession through the impressive gates and up the long driveway as the astonishing estate comes into view, with the dramatic San Jacinto mountain range as a background; the beautiful, clear morning light of the desert revealing one of the most important collections of Impressionist and Post-Impressionist paintings in the world; and the conversations of some of the most powerful figures of the last century gathered to discuss the affairs of the day over an ever-changing, elegantly set table carefully orchestrated by Mrs. Annenberg herself. This was heady stuff indeed!

Thankfully, the Sunnylands legacy continues to this day. The estate and its grounds remain a destination for presidents, foreign dignitaries, and diplomats alike, a venue for discussion and reflection, while becoming a public destination for ninety thousand visitors a year. The grant-making Annenberg Foundation, as well as the Annenberg Foundation Trust at Sunnylands, are a testament to the Annenbergs' philanthropy and extraordinary vision. As the photographs and text in this wonderful book by Janice Lyle can attest, the estate is as visually arresting today as it was when the Annenbergs greeted their illustrious guests. Thanks to their generosity and foresight, Sunnylands will continue to inspire other visionaries from all walks of life for many years to come.

Michael S. Smith
May 2016

MEET THE ANNENBERGS

Above Photographs and letters displayed in the Room of Memories record important moments in the Annenbergs' lives.

Opposite Was Walter Annenberg's personality truly captured by artist Andrew Wyeth in this portrait painted in 1978? Although Leonore thought Walter looked stern here, Wyeth said, "There is nothing of the cream puff about Walter."

Overleaf Wood silhouettes of Leonore and Walter hang on the doors to the women's and men's locker rooms.

Walter and Leonore Annenberg were often called the greatest philanthropists of their generation. They donated their billion-dollar art collection to the Metropolitan Museum of Art in New York and gave hundreds of millions to cultural, educational, and medical institutions, capping a lifetime of success in business and public service.

Their circle of friends included presidents of the United States, British royalty, captains of industry, and Hollywood celebrities. Notably, Walter served with distinction as United States Ambassador to the Court of St. James's under President Richard Nixon, and Leonore held the rank of ambassador as Chief of Protocol for President Ronald Reagan.

Walter Hubert Annenberg was born in Milwaukee, Wisconsin on March 13, 1908. The only son of Moses and Sadie Annenberg, he grew up with seven sisters. Moses and his family had emigrated from Eastern Europe in the 1880s. After the turn of the century, Moses worked in circulation for William Randolph Hearst and later built his own successful publishing company, which included the *Daily Racing Form*, *Philadelphia Inquirer*, and Nationwide Wire Service.

Moses and Sadie moved their family to New York in 1920 and enrolled Walter in the private Peddie School in New Jersey. Walter graduated in 1927 and started his lifetime of philanthropy by funding a new running track at the school.

Next, he attended the University of Pennsylvania's Wharton School, where he studied business before joining his father's publishing company, Triangle Publications, Inc.

As a young publishing executive, Walter frequently traveled to California, where he spent time with Hollywood studio executives and developed lifelong friendships with Ronald Reagan and others in the burgeoning entertainment business. Following his father's death in 1942, Walter inherited Triangle Publications, Inc. As chief executive, he transformed the company into one of the communication world's great powers. He introduced *Seventeen* magazine, the first major American magazine to focus on young women in America. He began buying television stations in 1948 and then developed a plan to publish a combination of national and local listings of television programs. *TV Guide*, launched in 1953, went on to become the most widely distributed weekly magazine in the nation, printing a billion copies a year at its peak. Walter also showed his genius for anticipating trends in television when he launched *Bandstand*, a live music and dance show for teenagers, in 1953, and ultimately went national with *Dick Clark's American Bandstand* in 1957.

Leonore Cohn was born in New York on February 20, 1918. Her mother died when she was seven years old, and from the age of eleven, she was raised in Hollywood by her aunt and uncle, Rose and Harry Cohn, who was head of Columbia Pictures. A 1940 Stanford graduate, she met Walter in 1950 through her friend Harriet Simon Deutsch. The couple were married in 1951, each having two children from previous marriages.

The newlyweds lived in Wynnewood, Pennsylvania, where Leonore redid their estate, Inwood, with help from the Los Angeles designer William Haines, creating exquisite traditional interiors with eighteenth-century English and French furniture.

Together, Walter and Leonore shared a passion for art collecting, which connected them to the museum world on the East Coast. Their pursuit of Impressionist and Post-Impressionist masterpieces began in 1951 and was a source of mutual interest throughout their marriage. Rather than using curators or professional art advisors,

the Annenbergs made their selections from a small group of New York galleries, always maintaining the highest standards. "I am a nut on quality, on QUALITY!" Walter told the *Washington Post*.

Art and music were central to their cultural lives in Philadelphia, and support of education was a major interest. Walter was recognized for his early commitment to public education with the George Foster Peabody Award—broadcast journalism's highest honor—for his *University of the Air*, which offered college courses on his television station WFIL.

During the 1950s, the Annenbergs began spending time each winter in the Palm Springs area, usually staying at the La Quinta Resort. Leonore, a Californian at heart, wanted to build a winter home in the California desert. In 1963, they decided to develop the site that was to become Sunnylands in Rancho Mirage.

Walter's role as publisher of the *Philadelphia Inquirer* gave him visibility and political clout. He considered himself an "independent Republican" and played an ever-increasing role in state and national politics. He supported the Eisenhower/Nixon ticket in 1952 and later donated a portrait of Benjamin Franklin to the White House when asked by Jacqueline Kennedy. In the 1964 election, Walter endorsed Democrat Lyndon Johnson for president rather than the Republican Barry Goldwater. Then in 1968, his friend Richard Nixon made a second run for the presidency and won. Walter's close ties to Nixon led to his appointment as Ambassador to the Court of St. James's, a position he held from 1969 until 1974.

The Annenbergs' diplomatic service resulted in lifelong friendships with the British royal family and a deep understanding of the importance of cultural diplomacy. In 1976, the Queen conferred upon Walter an honorary KBE (Knight Commander of the Most Excellent Order of the British Empire) and, in 2004, upon Leonore an honorary CBE (Commander of the Most Excellent Order of the British Empire).

The Annenbergs maintained a close friendship with Ronald and Nancy Reagan following his election as Governor of California in 1966. Later, Walter played an instrumental role in introducing Reagan to Margaret Thatcher, the rising star in

Britain's Conservative Party. Following the 1980 presidential election, Reagan called upon Leonore to serve as Chief of Protocol in his administration. Every year during the Reagan presidency (1981–89), the Reagans attended the annual New Year's Eve party at Sunnylands, where as many as a hundred Annenberg friends celebrated the holiday. It was also Reagan's annual outing on the golf course. These weekends led to other working meetings with the President and members of his cabinet at Sunnylands.

An intuitive businessman with a skill for timing, Walter Annenberg sold his publishing portfolio to Rupert Murdoch's News Corporation for $3.2 billion in 1988. Following the sale of their company, the Annenbergs dedicated their lives to philanthropy. Over the next five years, their contributions included $50 million to the United Negro College Fund, $500 million to K–12 public education, and a $365 million gift to the University of Southern California, the University of Pennsylvania, Harvard University, and the Peddie School. "Education is the only answer," he said. "It's the glue that holds civilization together. Without it, we would go back to the Dark Ages."

The gift of the Annenbergs' Impressionist and Post-Impressionist art collection to the Metropolitan Museum of Art in New York was the largest single donation to any museum in a half-century. The collection included more than fifty paintings by, among others, Paul Cézanne, Edgar Degas, Paul Gauguin, Claude Monet, Pierre-Auguste Renoir, and Vincent van Gogh.

The decision to create the Annenberg Retreat at Sunnylands as a private operating foundation represented their final major charitable contribution. The Annenberg Foundation Trust at Sunnylands, which operates the Annenberg Retreat at Sunnylands, is governed exclusively by the children and grandchildren of both Walter and Leonore. The Annenberg Foundation, which continues the family's tradition of inspired philanthropy, operates under the stewardship of Walter's daughter and three of her children.

After fifty-one years of marriage, Walter died in 2002. Leonore passed away in 2009. Sunnylands remains a reflection of a particular moment and vision in architecture, interior design, and social history—the midcentury modern American version of a great English country house.

Opposite Walter and Leonore near the three-hole golf course at Inwood, their Pennsylvania home, in the early 1950s.

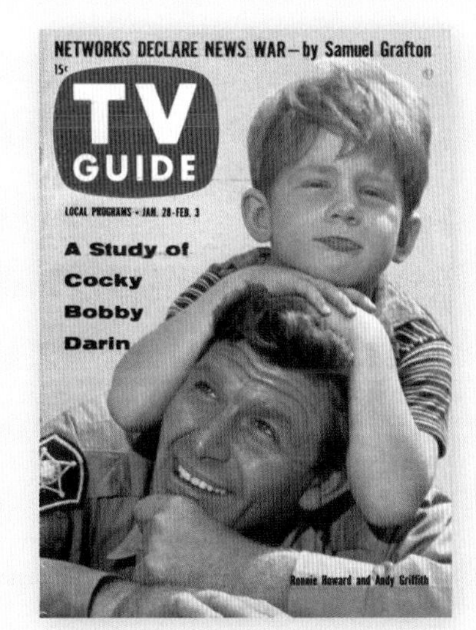

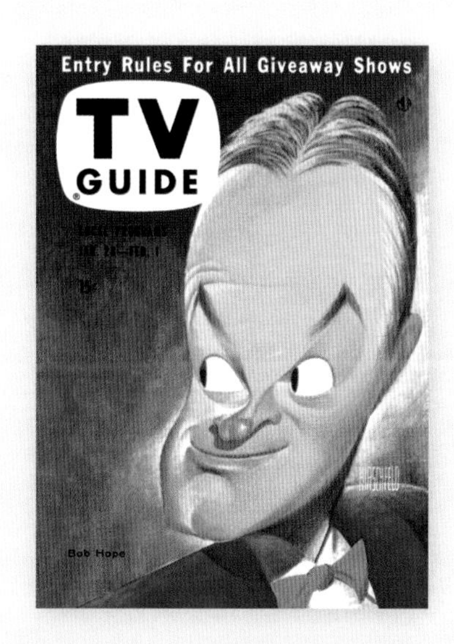

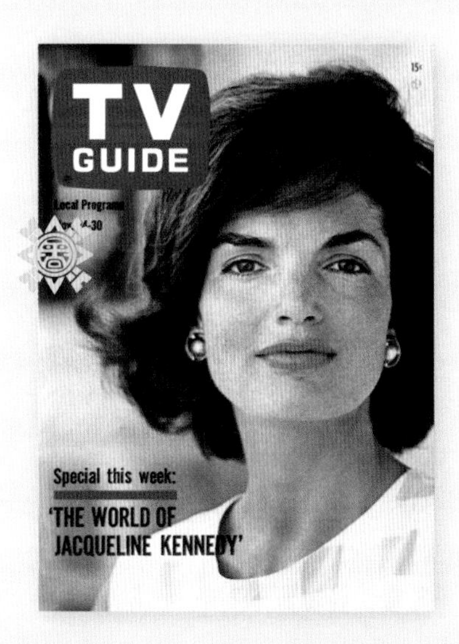

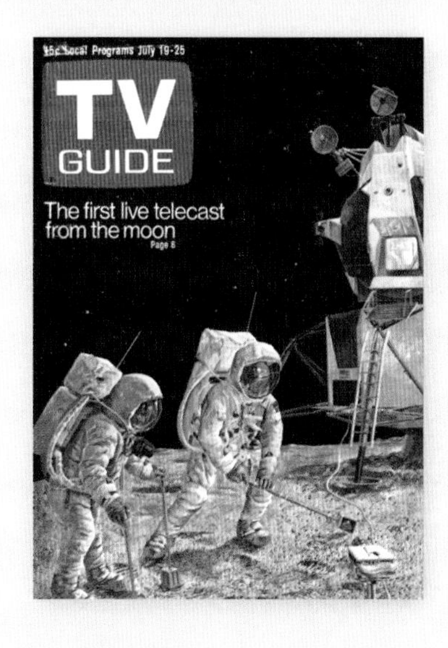

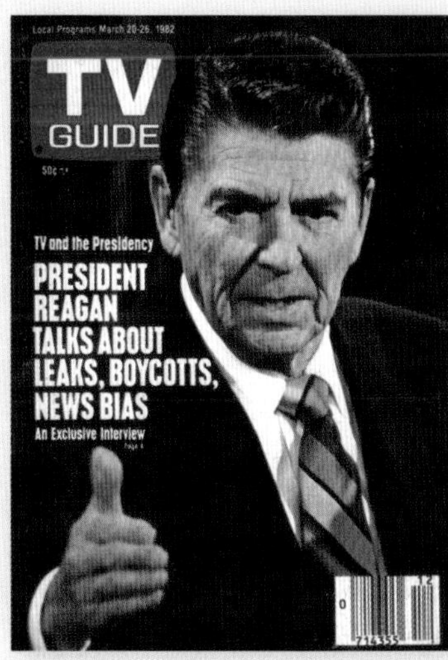

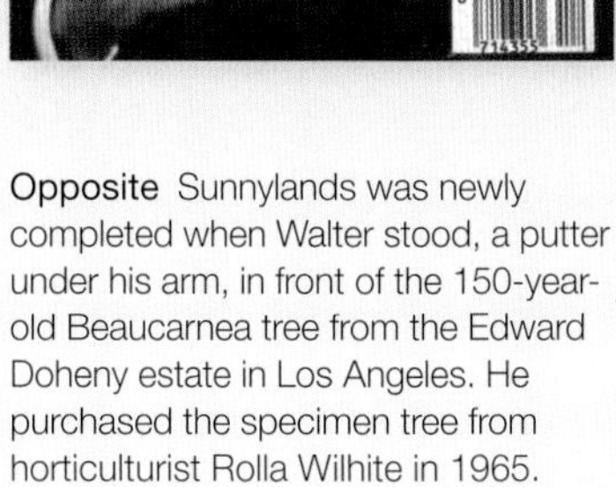

Opposite Sunnylands was newly completed when Walter stood, a putter under his arm, in front of the 150-year-old Beaucarnea tree from the Edward Doheny estate in Los Angeles. He purchased the specimen tree from horticulturist Rolla Wilhite in 1965.

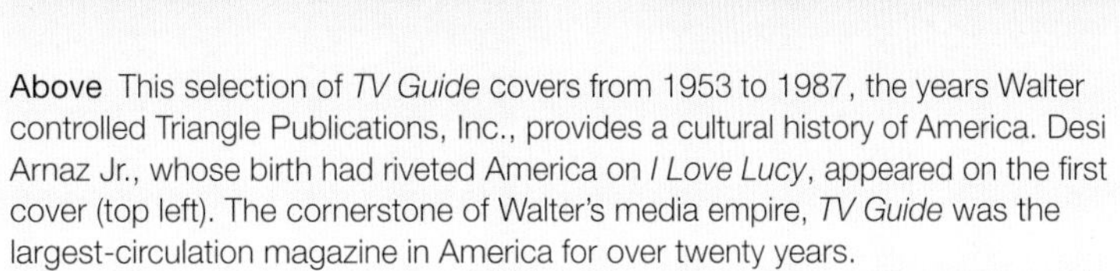

Above This selection of *TV Guide* covers from 1953 to 1987, the years Walter controlled Triangle Publications, Inc., provides a cultural history of America. Desi Arnaz Jr., whose birth had riveted America on *I Love Lucy*, appeared on the first cover (top left). The cornerstone of Walter's media empire, *TV Guide* was the largest-circulation magazine in America for over twenty years.

In 1968, newspaper columnist and photographer Gloria Etting memorialized her visit to Sunnylands by sending a scrapbook of photographs taken during her stay. These images capture Leonore's sense of style and her delight with the furnishings and sculpture in her new home. Note the original living room furniture arrangement, with the sofas winged.

Opposite This detail of the lace bodice of a couture Pierre Balmain gown reflects Leonore's penchant for pink, yellow, and green—colors seen throughout Sunnylands.

Above Pink, yellow, and green—and a beautiful day for flying—are captured in this 1967 photograph of Leonore boarding the Annenbergs' private Gulfstream aircraft.

DESIGNING SUNNYLANDS

The story goes that the Annenbergs were playing golf at Tamarisk Country Club in Rancho Mirage when they looked at an area of open desert adjacent to the course and decided to build a house and private golf course there. "Every time we came down the fourteenth fairway, we could see this big mound of sand because there was nothing here then, nothing," said Leonore. Beginning in 1963, Walter began acquiring large parcels of land—at one point the Annenbergs owned nearly 950 acres in what is now Rancho Mirage—and chose to develop two hundred acres adjacent to Rio del Sol (now Bob Hope Drive) and Wonder Palms Road (now Frank Sinatra Drive) as their desert oasis. The Annenbergs had no interest in creating a traditional house like the one in Wynnewood and looked westward for a California architect.

Good friends Armand and Harriet Deutsch had remodeled a house in Holmby Hills in 1960 using A. Quincy Jones as the architect and William Haines as the interior designer. In 1950, that same team had also developed a house for neighbors Sidney and Frances Brody to much acclaim. So in January 1963, the Annenbergs contacted William Haines and asked him to reassemble the team to work with them. Haines

Above The egg crate–coffered ceiling detail was not cast in concrete, but built with wood and plaster.

Opposite William Haines stands in the wide-open desert in March 1964 as the Annenbergs begin the transformation of two hundred acres of sand into an oasis.

Overleaf Architecture writer Esther McCoy said of A. Quincy Jones, "He liked a serious roof."

was a firm believer that "the interior decorator, the landscape gardener, and the architect should all be consulted in the beginning. The three should be hired as a unit and work together."

Archibald Quincy Jones was an established Southern California architect who opened a firm in partnership with Frederick Earl Emmons in Los Angeles in 1951. Jones was actively engaged in midcentury modern design through his work on houses built by developer Joseph Eichler, his Case Study House #24 for *Arts & Architecture* magazine, and his commercial work. His role as a professor of architecture at the University of Southern California and later dean of its School of Architecture (1975–78) gave him a prominent place in Southern California architectural circles.

The first drawings from A. Quincy Jones, submitted in August 1963, reflected the Annenbergs' request that the house have a Mayan theme. The term "Mayan" is used loosely—Walter said that it seemed an appropriate style since the house would be in California adjacent to Mexico's wealth of Pre-Columbian history. The Annenbergs visited Mexico in 1967, so at this early stage in the project, they were discussing the Mayan style based on photographs they had seen of Chichén Itzá and Uxmal. There was some precedent for this idea in Frank Lloyd Wright's 1921 Hollyhock House and 1924 Ennis House, both in Los Angeles. In addition, Latin American modernist architects like Oscar Niemeyer, who was building Brasilia, were much in vogue in the 1960s, and Jones may have been influenced by some of the more organic qualities of their buildings. Jones's interpretation of a Mayan theme can be seen in his first drawing, with its three pyramidal-shaped roofs, battered walls used throughout, and lava-stone walls.

The Annenbergs very much wanted a house that would be open to the outdoors. Jones achieved that sense of openness and relaxed living with a surprising diagonal entrance, a central garden also on an oblique axis, partition walls that don't rise to the ceiling, and an egg crate–coffered ceiling connecting the interior and exterior. Wide expanses of glass blur the line between indoors and outdoors, pulling the green landscape inside the residence.

Jones's first drawing for the main house was revised following a meeting with the Annenbergs in September 1963. The requested aviary was deleted, two of the three pyramidal roofs were removed and replaced by flat roofs, and the orientation on the site was shifted to improve the views. The central atrium, under the only remaining pyramidal roof, became more prominent. The new plan included two separate structures: a main house containing a single large space designated as the atrium, living, and dining rooms; with a wing for the master suite and second bedroom and a wing that included the kitchen, staff areas, and billiard room; and a guest building featuring two bedrooms and a shared den. By January 1964, the house design was essentially finished and the Annenbergs ordered a model to be made. While the main house was under construction, three modest houses, called cottages, and a maintenance yard, also designed by Jones, were built. The Annenbergs occasionally stayed at one of the cottages when visiting the developing estate.

By fall 1964, the basement was excavated and the steel frame of the approximately 25,000-square-foot house rose. The rough enclosure of the house was completed by May 1965, and by late September, the house was nearly finished, except for the glazing. Among the specialized materials used were sandblasted redwood painted celadon green for interior walls, lava stone for exterior facades and interior walls, and rose marble for flooring.

The experience of entering Sunnylands is not like that of a chateau or stately home or even a traditional house. There is no entry hall.

Left Architect A. Quincy Jones (1917–1979) designed many enduring landmarks in Southern California, including the Annenberg School for Communication at the University of Southern California.

Below An early watercolor collage by architect Kaz Nomura, who worked in Jones's office, depicts three pyramidal roofs.

Opposite above Jones's initial plan from August 1963, delivered to the Annenbergs in September for discussion and review.

Opposite below The site plan from August 1963 shows Jones's early thinking about the driveway, interconnecting lakes, golf course, and the use of eucalyptus, olive, oleander, and tamarisk trees for shade and wind control.

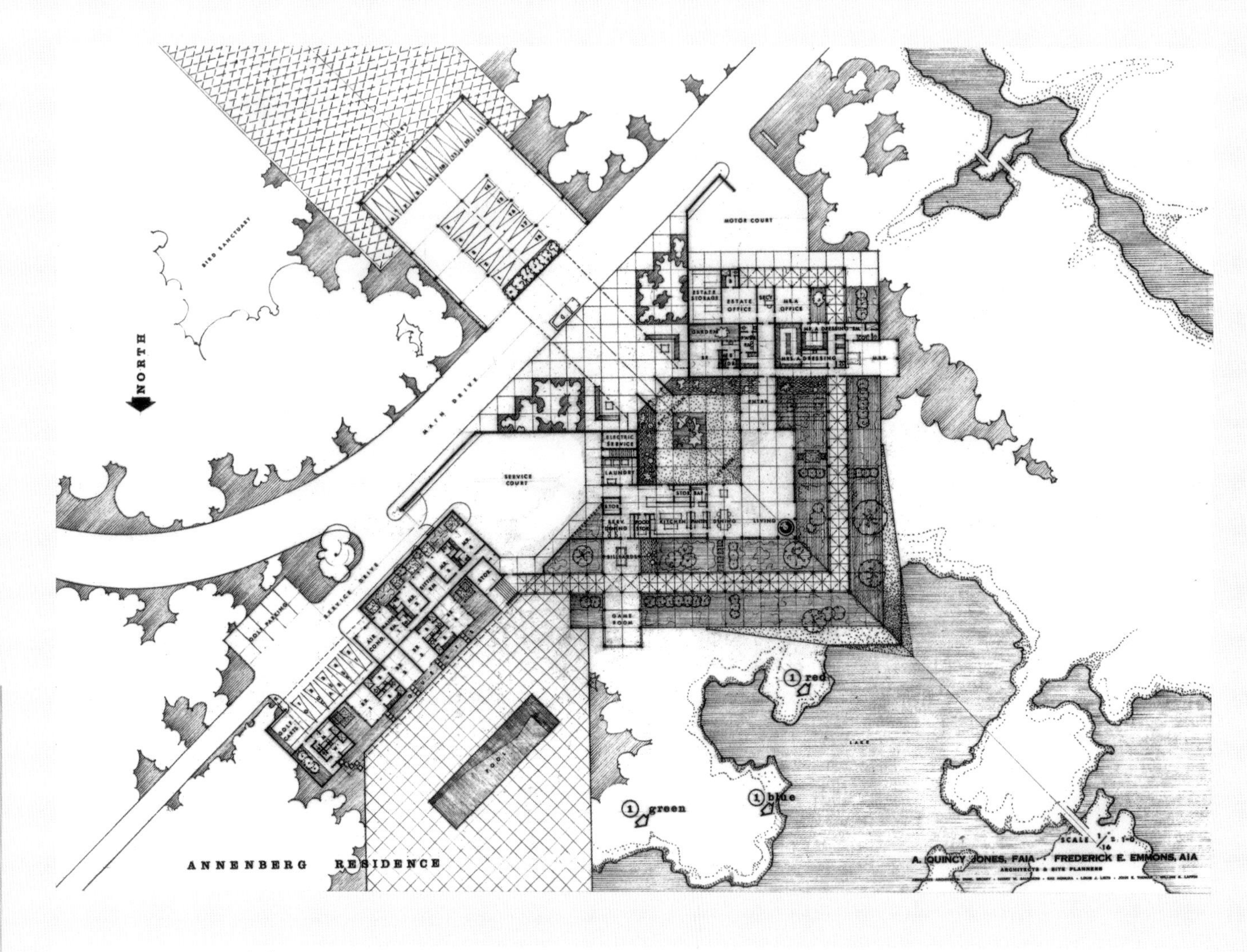
NORTH
MOTOR COURT
ESTATE STORAGE
ESTATE OFFICE
M&A OFFICE
MAIN DRIVE
SERVICE COURT
ELECTRIC SERVICE
LAUNDRY
ENTRY
LIVING
GAME ROOM
SERVICE DRIVE
LAKE
1 red
1 green
1 blue
SCALE 1/16" = 1'-0"
ANNENBERG RESIDENCE
A. QUINCY JONES, FAIA · FREDERICK E. EMMONS, AIA
ARCHITECTS & SITE PLANNERS

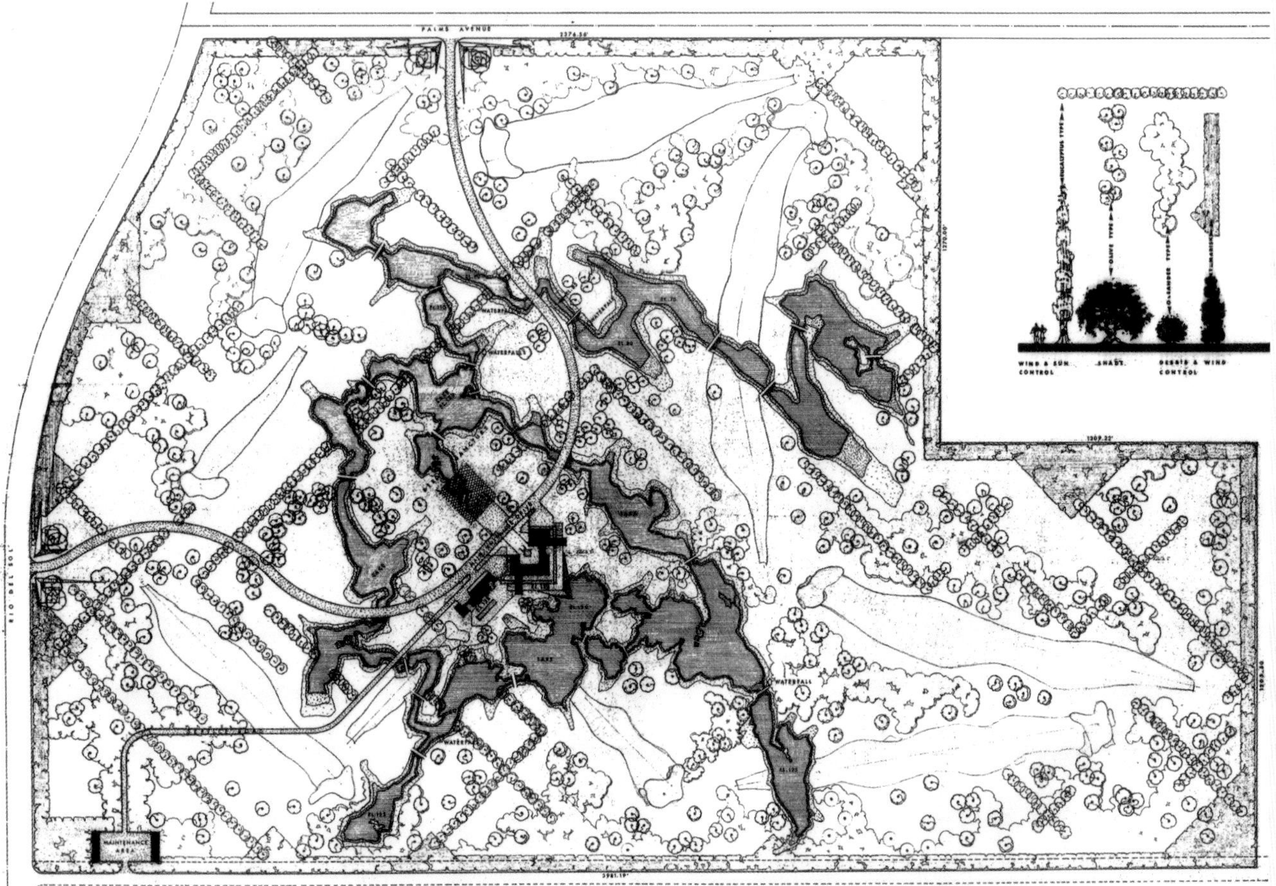
WATERFALL
MAINTENANCE AREA
WIND & SUN CONTROL
SHADE
DEBRIS & WIND CONTROL
ANNENBERG RESIDENCE
A. QUINCY JONES, FAIA · FREDERICK E. EMMONS, AIA
ARCHITECTS & SITE PLANNERS

Movement does not follow a formal or even obvious flow. The visitor circulates freely, and a sense of informality and openness dominates. This aesthetic reflects the collaboration of architect, designer, and client. Jones's midcentury modern architectural style, with its exposed steel columns, was softened considerably by the Hollywood Regency furnishings designed by William Haines, and enlivened by the Annenbergs' Impressionist and Post-Impressionist paintings, modern sculpture, and decorative art collections.

The Annenbergs officially occupied the house beginning March 6, 1966, and quickly began welcoming friends to the estate. Reflecting the Mayan theme, an image of a yellow sun god on a white flag was flown when they were in residence.

Although there have been changes over the years, they are not easily detected, and the house looks much the same today as it did when it was finished. One difference is that the house had a garden quality when it was first completed, with planters below the lava stone walls in the atrium and more plantings throughout the house. After Walter served as Ambassador to the Court of St. James's in London, the Annenbergs decided to rethink the informality of the house. Walter "wanted the house to be formal, but not too formal." They also wanted to bring their paintings to Sunnylands from their primary residence in Pennsylvania. To accommodate the paintings, the planters at the base of the lava stone walls were removed, skylights sealed off, and ceiling lights added. This involved extending the rose marble floors all the way to the wall, enlarging the usable floor space as well. This change had a significant visual impact as the sense of garden living that had been such an important part of Jones's original design was significantly reduced.

From 1974 to 1977, Harry Saunders, an associate in Jones's and Emmons's office during the original construction of Sunnylands and by that time in practice for himself, was hired by the Annenbergs. He provided a gallery for their new Steuben glass collection and three additional guest suites in a new guest wing. Outdoor elements, such as the Chinese Pavilion and the First Nations totem pole, were added at this time as well.

Saunders also created a separate dining room. The dining room was originally adjacent to the atrium—between the indoor plants surrounding

ANNENBERG RESIDENCE

Rodin's *Eve* and the outdoor upper terrace with its blooming bougainvillea. In 1977 the original billiard room was enlarged into the new formal dining room where the Annenbergs would entertain up to twenty-two people at two tables. The only other significant change to the house occurred in 2007, when the Inwood Room replaced an indoor swimming pool to create space for a selection of antiques from the newly closed Main Line house.

The Annenberg Foundation Trust at Sunnylands undertook a major restoration of the house in 2010 to 2012 following Leonore Annenberg's death. The restoration followed the basic principles of: do no harm; make the house safe for public access; and increase the efficiency and sustainability of mechanical and other systems. Working with the architecture firm Frederick Fisher & Partners and the preservation consultants at Historic Resources Group, the Sunnylands staff shaped the restoration in two ways. Any aspects of the physical space that required change were to be brought back to the original design intent of the 1960s where possible. If the space was the result of 1970s changes, then it would be returned to its 1970s configuration, which was closely aligned with Sunnylands' period of greatest cultural significance—the 1980s Reagan presidency.

Upgrades included replacing all the glass in the house with code-required tempered glass and repainting the interior using original paint samples. The house met 1965 earthquake standards but not 2012 standards, so seismic retrofitting was done. The biggest challenge was the replacement of the iconic pink pyramidal roof tiles. White cement tiles, which were painted pink every three to five years, needed to be replaced. Continuing the practice of painting the roof, which trapped moisture and degraded the tiles, seemed wrong. Instead eight thousand integrally colored "peach parfait" tiles were produced in eighty different molds with distinct brushstrokes, so that the look was identical to the original.

There is no other midcentury modern house on this scale or of this integrity that reflects such a golden moment in California history. Architectural historian David DeLong has said that Jones created at Sunnylands "a major example of mid-twentieth-century architecture specific to America, a modern architecture responsive to its occupants as individuals and reflective of place as a determinant of design."

This January 1964 elevation drawing depicts the main house and guest wing along with various elements that would never be built.

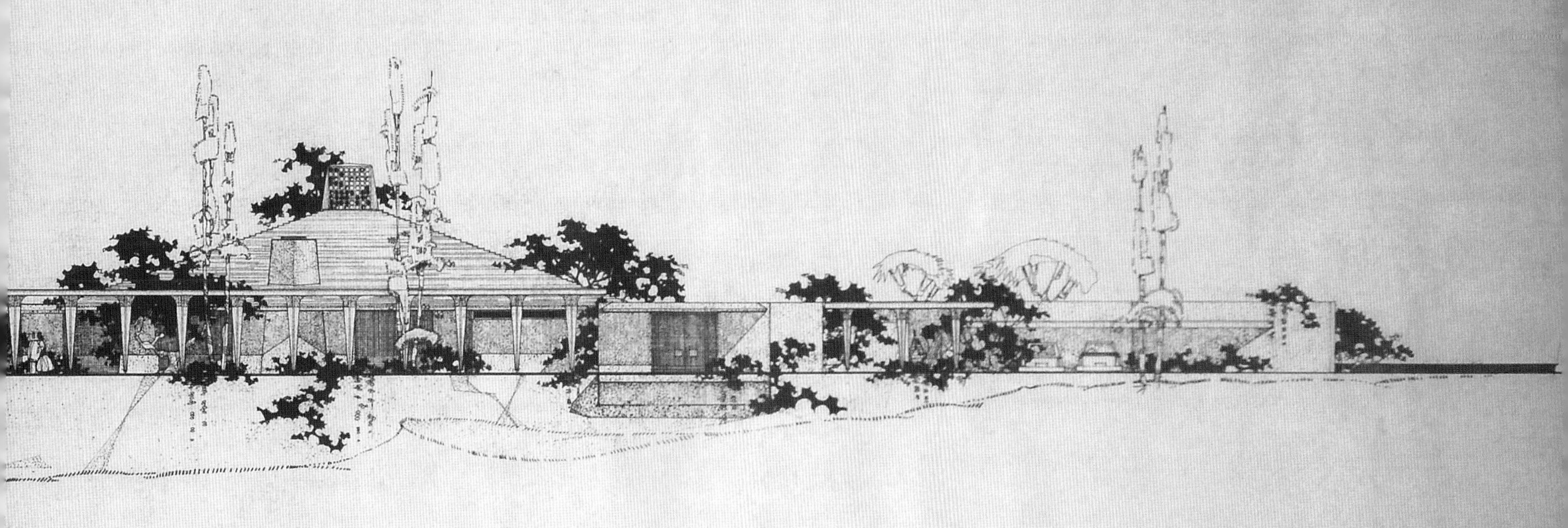

Walter and Leonore were active participants in the design and construction of Sunnylands. Here they are seen on various site visits in 1964. William Haines, bottom right, would have been sixty-four years old at the time.

Images taken during construction show the house taking shape, the logos of suppliers, and, left, the model of the main house and guest wing commissioned in January 1964.

Opposite below The Annenbergs stand on a viewing platform with their architect to determine the siting, elevation, and orientation of the house.

Overleaf The floor plan of the main house and guest wing as they are today, drawn by architect Harry Saunders in 2007.

Pages 42–43 Renowned architectural photographer Julius Shulman photographed Sunnylands in 2007 for an exhibition of his work at the Palm Springs Art Museum, immortalizing the trees in their topiary form.

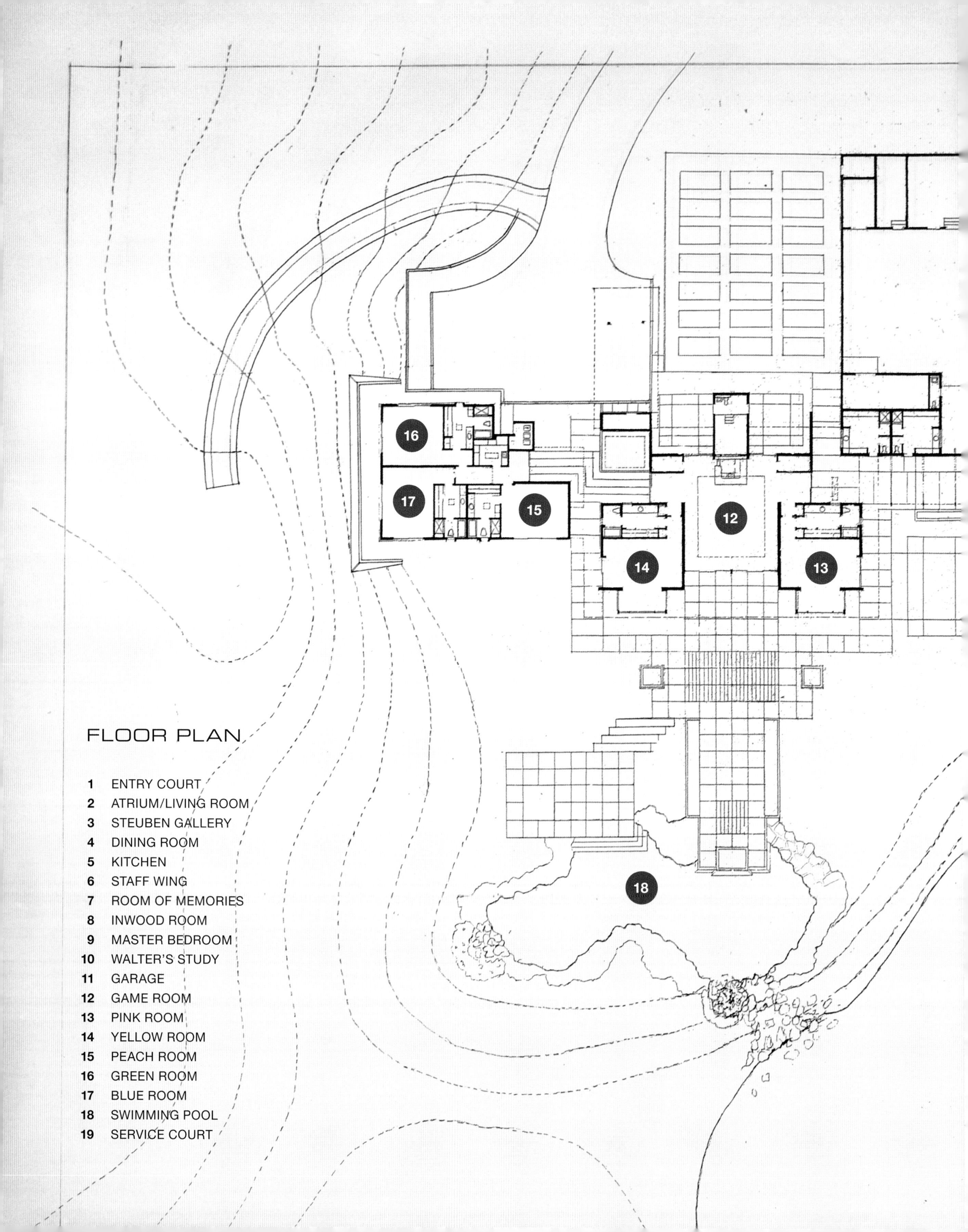
16
17
15
12
14
13
18
FLOOR PLAN
1 ENTRY COURT
2 ATRIUM/LIVING ROOM
3 STEUBEN GALLERY
4 DINING ROOM
5 KITCHEN
6 STAFF WING
7 ROOM OF MEMORIES
8 INWOOD ROOM
9 MASTER BEDROOM
10 WALTER'S STUDY
11 GARAGE
12 GAME ROOM
13 PINK ROOM
14 YELLOW ROOM
15 PEACH ROOM
16 GREEN ROOM
17 BLUE ROOM
18 SWIMMING POOL
19 SERVICE COURT

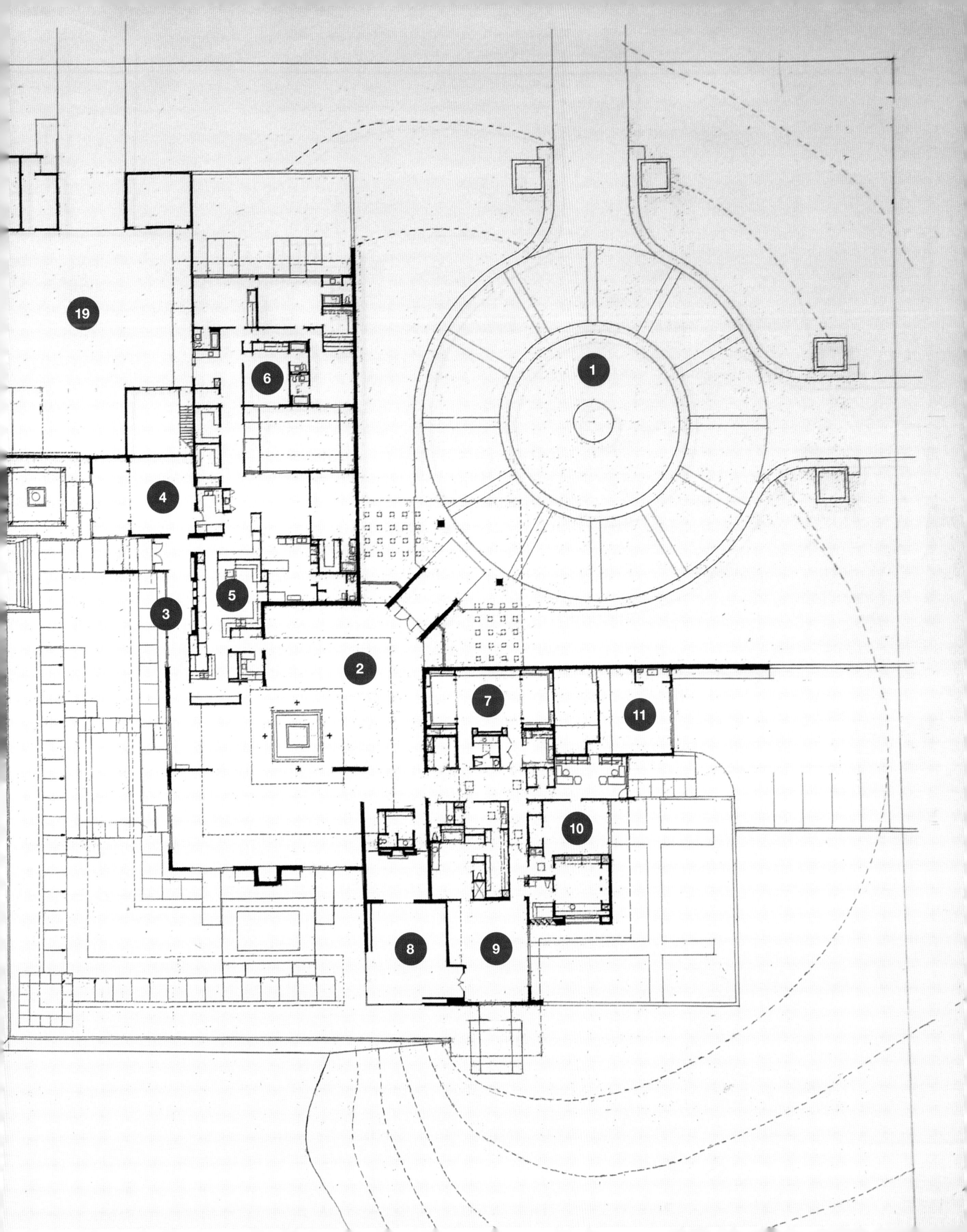
19
1
6
4
5
3
2
7
11
10
8
9

William Haines HIS SIGNATURES

Peter Schifando, president of William Haines Designs in Los Angeles, explains some of the frequently seen trademarks that make a William Haines room unmistakable.

THE UNICORN LEG Haines always pursued the extra, unexpected detail. The silhouette of this gondola sofa would have been drama enough for another designer, but Haines heightened its sense of luxury—as he often did—by wrapping the metal frame in spiraling cream leather, like the spiraling horn of the legendary unicorn.

THE LOW SILHOUETTE Haines tried to show women's dresses at their best and encourage "long-leg posing" through the use of low-slung seating. The seat height of this grouping is sixteen inches, compared to a more traditional nineteen inches.

THE PEDESTAL TABLE Haines carefully considered people's behaviors in his work. He always preferred a pedestal dining table, which—with no legs to get in the way—allowed chairs to be placed and moved freely, and encouraged closeness and conversation.

TRAPUNTO QUILTING Haines often made upholstered furniture more personal with exquisite, hand-quilted trapunto designs in relief—an art rarely seen today. The motif on this living room stool makes reference to Leonore's love of flowers.

BISCUIT TUFTING Haines had an affinity for the strong, modern geometry of box or "biscuit" tufting, even using this motif on his own sofa. That one detail makes this otherwise clean-lined chair seem sumptuous.

THE MUSEUM-MOUNT LAMP
Haines sourced many Chinese objets d'art to be used as lamps. Although the fashion of the times was to drill holes in antique ceramics, ruining their value, Haines would build his lamps around them using non-invasive bases. At Sunnylands you can see turquoise foo dogs and elephants, mustard-glazed oxen, and twenty-inch-tall cloisonné vases as lamps, often in pairs.

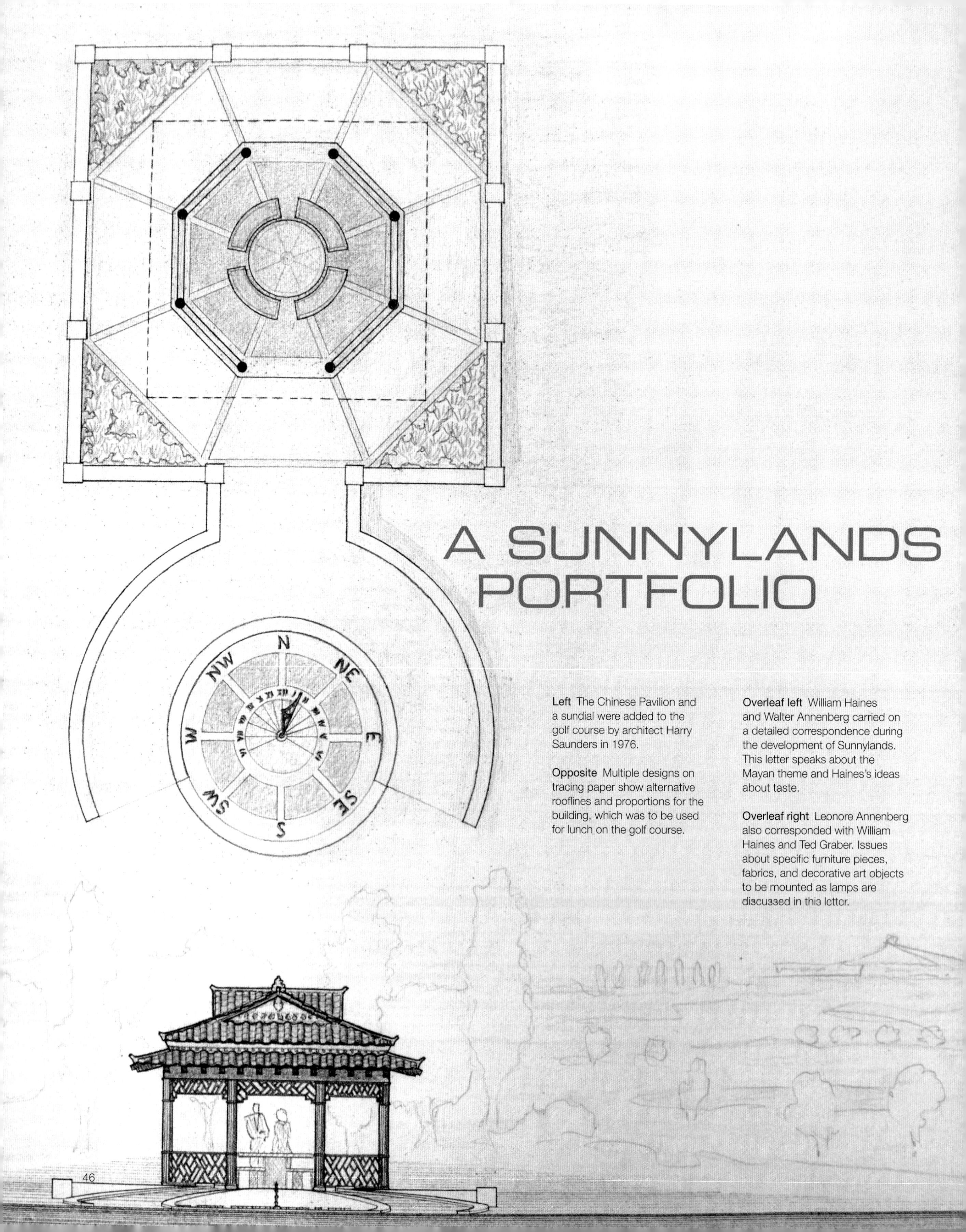

A SUNNYLANDS PORTFOLIO

Left The Chinese Pavilion and a sundial were added to the golf course by architect Harry Saunders in 1976.

Opposite Multiple designs on tracing paper show alternative rooflines and proportions for the building, which was to be used for lunch on the golf course.

Overleaf left William Haines and Walter Annenberg carried on a detailed correspondence during the development of Sunnylands. This letter speaks about the Mayan theme and Haines's ideas about taste.

Overleaf right Leonore Annenberg also corresponded with William Haines and Ted Graber. Issues about specific furniture pieces, fabrics, and decorative art objects to be mounted as lamps are discussed in this letter.

william haines inc.
designs
446 s. canon dr.
beverly hills
california

October 7, 1963

Mr. Walter H. Annenberg
The Philadelphia Inquirer
Philadelphia 1, Pa.

Dear Walter:

Yours of September 30th received. I have been away from the office, thus the delay in my answer.

When we were in Philadelphia, and you asked what the period of the house was, I said it was suggestive of the Mayan architecture in Chichen-Itza in its retaining walls. Actually, this remark was not intended to identify or associate the architecture of your house with any particular style or period. I feel that it was Quincy's intent, and I most surely know it is mine that your house should definitely be as timeless as it can be, or as much as Jones can make it, and I can furnish it.

I do feel that architecture and design is a continuous chain of improvement and/or conception from the last period that is has evolved from to its current state. But there are basic principles that thread through all periods. From the first skin tent of primitive man to the glass birdcages that man shows his love of exhibitionism in today, the true facts are: a house must have a foundation, walls, and a roof. What takes place between or within these elements concerns the taste. There are two kinds of taste - good and bad. There is no integration here. Most people do not have taste, never know they don't have it, thus being extremely happy like all people who have not been exposed to beauty beyond the point of their noses. Then there are the exquisite few who do have taste. They can't explain why, but they know it; they can feel it, but can't touch it. It's like intangible fog you can see and feel it, but can't touch it.

I don't know what brought that on! I suppose I was trying to say that your house first should reflect yours and Lee's taste and interests which I can easily see are very inquisitive and catholic.

crestview 6-9632 cable address SENIAHS bradshaw 2-2584

william haines inc.
designs
446 s.canon dr.
beverly hills
california

May 18, 1964

Dear Lee:

Ted saved your letter to him for me to answer. I have just returned from travels in the south, but that is another story.

I had never any intention of putting a sideboard in the dining room. I thought the two refractory tables at either end of the room, one by the window and one by the center fountain of the atrium, would be used as a buffet table singly, or together. These tables are 9' long and 28" wide in a closed position. The tables open to 42" wide. One of these can carry an awful lot of food. All tables will have a lacquer bar -top finish which is the best protection we can make.

I have studied your suggestion of substituting the celadon damask for the off-white silk canvas covers on the sofa in front of the stone wall. I would like to call to your attention that this material is quilted in a trellage pattern and receives four pillows, two in pink silk canvas and two in celadon green silk canvas. This arrangement balances the other end of the room in colour. Then, too, the celadon draperies hang at the stone wall and I feel it would be a little too much celadon damask. However, if you really want these changes made, I will concur sadly, but I will concur. It will cause trouble as the celadon damask has been received and the other materials involved are now on the looms. Please let us know soon and I will do what you want.

We are getting along famously with all the furniture. Many pieces are now in work, others ordered. Materials are stacked high in our storage. When all materials have been received, we will make your swatch book.

I was most fortunate in buying in the south some superb pieces for lamps: a great pair of white porcelain de Paris vases incrusted with the most delicate three-dimentional white flowers for your bedroom.

I have Ch'ien Lung parrots, the most elegant Chinese hawk - all in that blue-green for the living room. I am going to take the elephants out of the atrium (find a substitution) and use them in the living room with the foregoing birds, and they, together with the dogs, will make the most amusing arrangement

crestview 6-9632 cable address SENIAHS bradshaw 2-2584

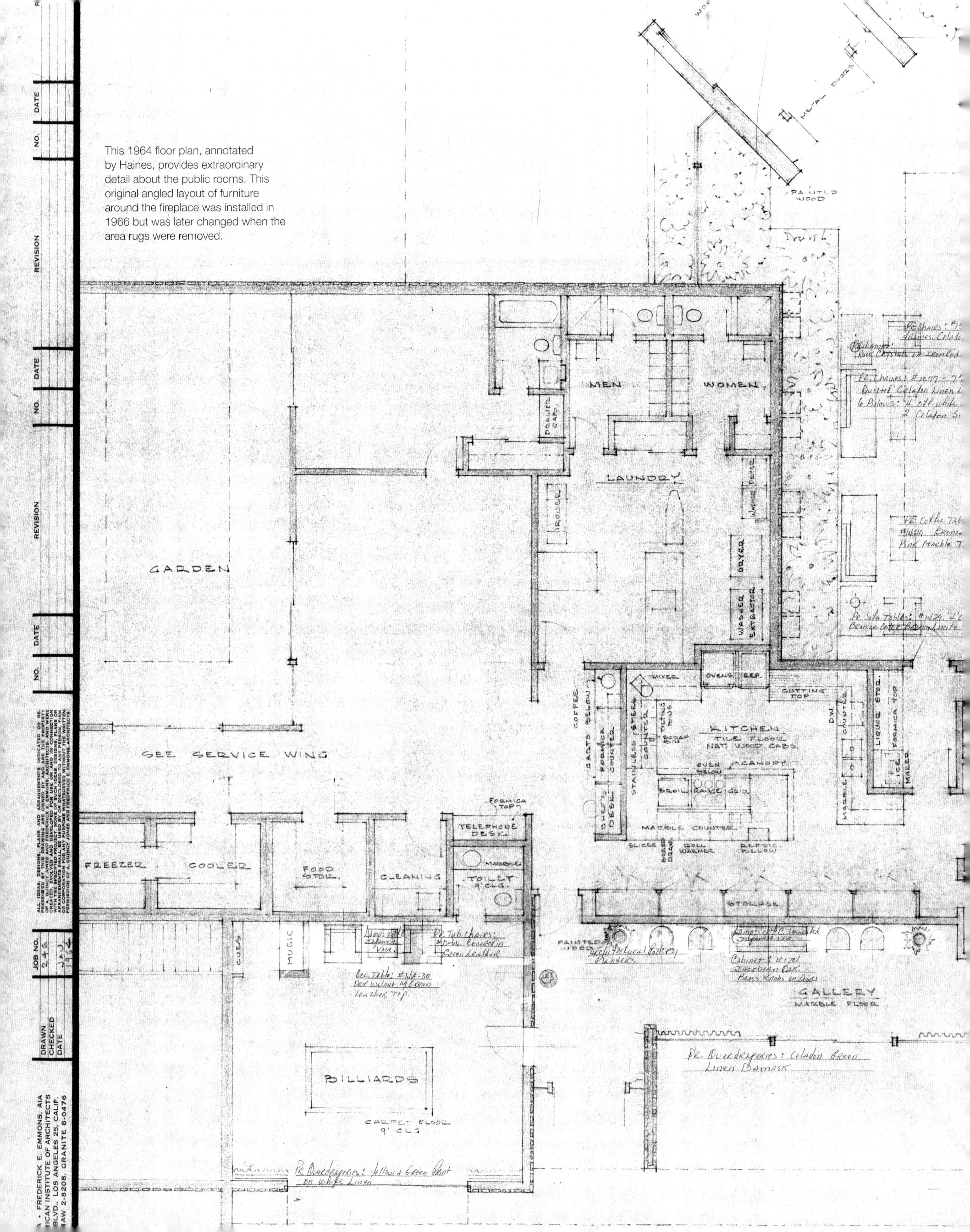

This 1964 floor plan, annotated by Haines, provides extraordinary detail about the public rooms. This original angled layout of furniture around the fireplace was installed in 1966 but was later changed when the area rugs were removed.

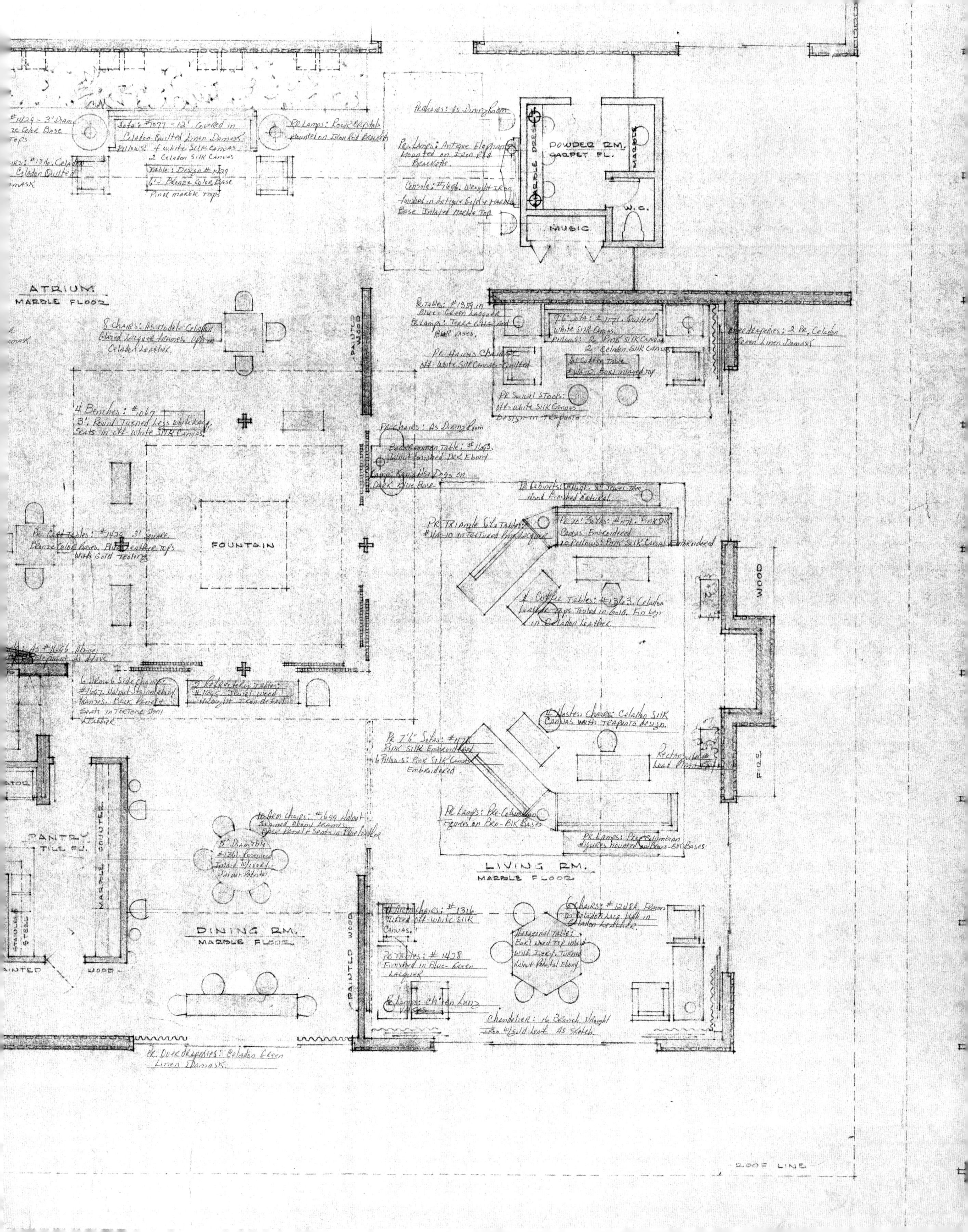

POWDER RM.
CARPET FL.
MUSIC
W.C.
ATRIUM
MARBLE FLOOR
FOUNTAIN
PAINTED WOOD
WOOD
FIRE
LIVING RM.
MARBLE FLOOR
DINING RM.
MARBLE FLOOR
PANTRY
TILE FL.
MARBLE COUNTER
ROOF LINE
Sofa: #1077 - 12'. Covered in Celadon Quilted Linen Damask
Pillows: 4 White SIlK Canvas 2 Celadon SIlK Canvas
Console: #1646. Wrought Iron finished in Antique Gold & Marble Base Inlayed Marble Top
Pr. Chairs: As Dining Room
4 Benches: #1067
Pr. Coffee Tables: #1363. Celadon Leather Tops Tooled in Gold. Fin Legs in Celadon Leather
Chandelier: 16 Branch. Wrought Iron w/ Gold Leaf. As Sketch.
Pr. Overdraperies: Celadon Green Linen Damask

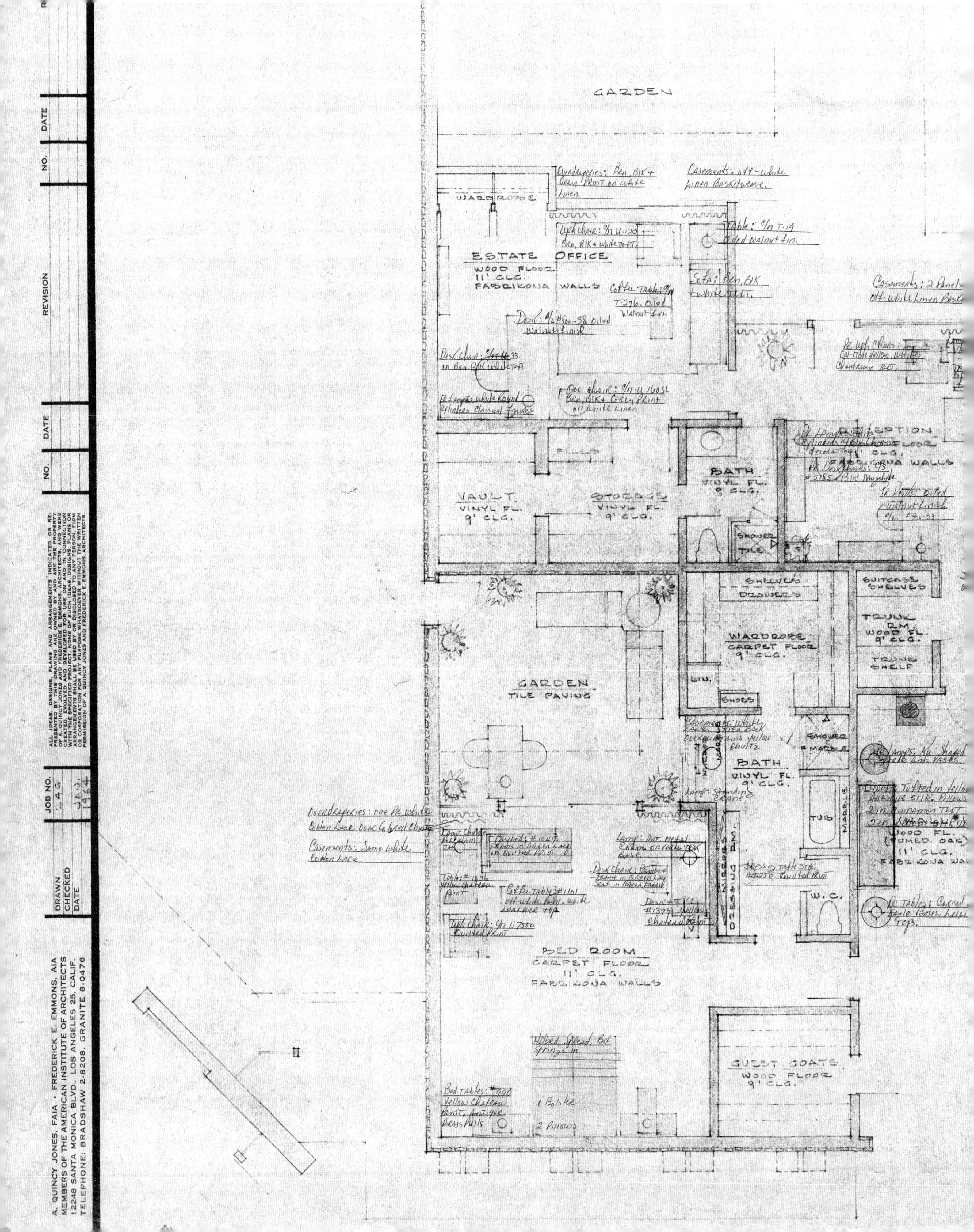

GARDEN
WARDROBE
ESTATE OFFICE
WOOD FLOOR
11' CLG.
FABRIKONA WALLS
Overdraperies: Ben, BlK + Grey Print on white Linen
Casements: off-white Linen Basketweave.
Sofa: Ben, BlK + white TEXT.
FILES
VAULT
VINYL FL.
9' CLG.
STORAGE
VINYL FL.
9' CLG.
BATH
VINYL FL.
9' CLG.
SHOWER
TILE
RECEPTION
FABRIKONA WALLS
SHELVES
DRAWERS
SUITCASE SHELVES
TRUNK RM.
WOOD FL.
9' CLG.
TRUNK SHELF
WARDROBE
CARPET FLOOR
9' CLG.
LIN.
SHOES
GARDEN
TILE PAVING
SHOWER
MARBLE
BATH
VINYL FL.
9' CLG.
TUB
MARBLE
W. C.
DRESSING RM.
MIRRORS
WOOD FL.
(FUMED OAK)
11' CLG.
Casements: Same white Cotton Lace.
BED ROOM
CARPET FLOOR
11' CLG.
FABRIKONA WALLS
GUEST COATS
WOOD FLOOR
9' CLG.
1 Bolster
2 Pillows
A. QUINCY JONES, FAIA • FREDERICK E. EMMONS, AIA
MEMBERS OF THE AMERICAN INSTITUTE OF ARCHITECTS
12248 SANTA MONICA BLVD. LOS ANGELES 25, CALIF.
TELEPHONE: BRADSHAW 2-8208, GRANITE 8-0476
DRAWN
CHECKED
DATE
JOB NO.
REVISION
NO.
DATE

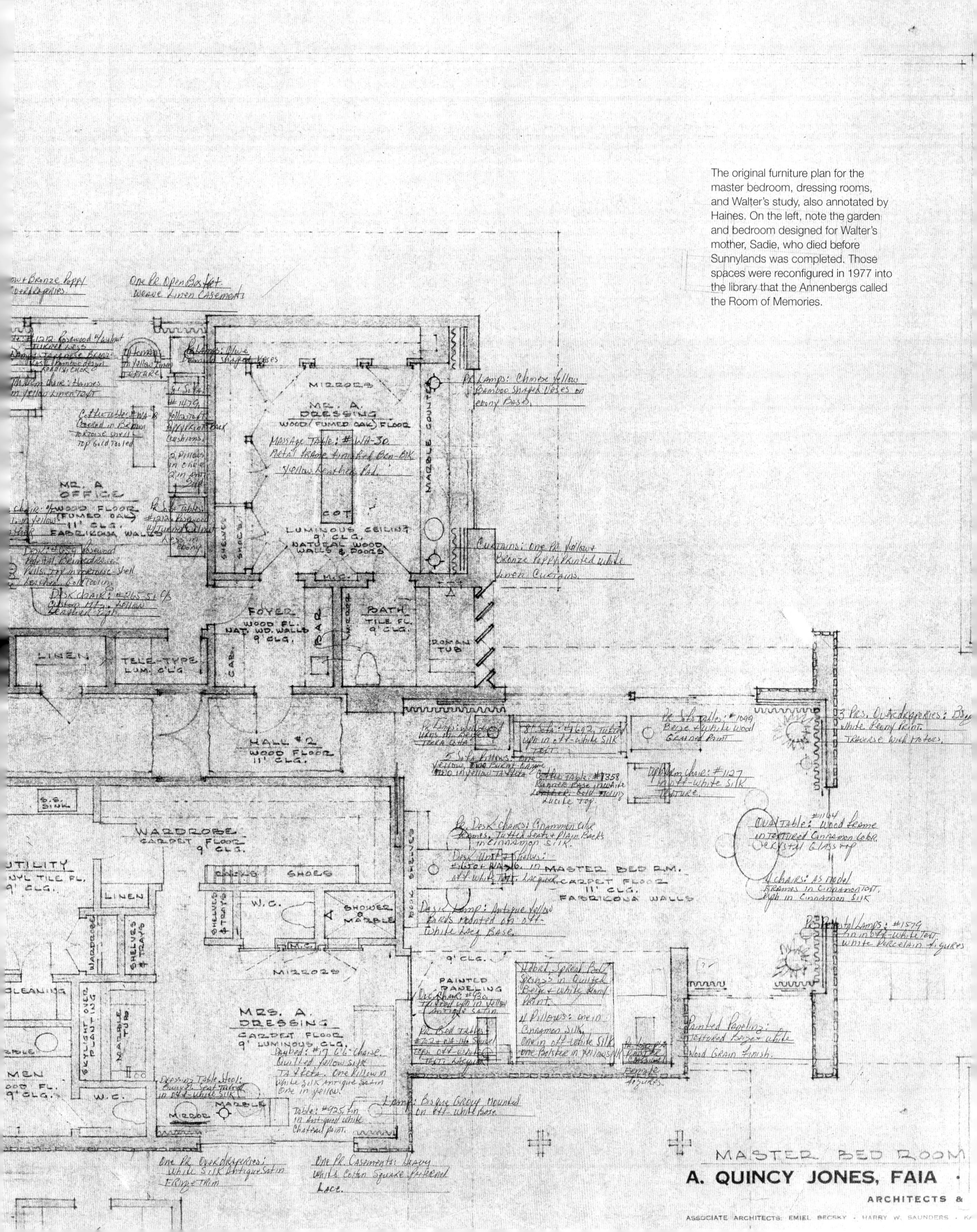

The original furniture plan for the master bedroom, dressing rooms, and Walter's study, also annotated by Haines. On the left, note the garden and bedroom designed for Walter's mother, Sadie, who died before Sunnylands was completed. Those spaces were reconfigured in 1977 into the library that the Annenbergs called the Room of Memories.

Haines's original watercolor drawing of an inlaid table with a pedestal base was accepted for the dining room.

This table was ultimately narrowed for the Tang funerary figures lining the atrium.

This coffee table was used in various finishes in the living room, master bedroom, and Walter's study.

Proposed tooled red leather tables were adapted for the master bedroom: the coffee table incorporated a Plexiglas top with white leather–wrapped trestle support, and the larger table was covered with a glass top on faux oak finish.

Gold-tooled chairs for the dining room ultimately had less decoration on the seats.

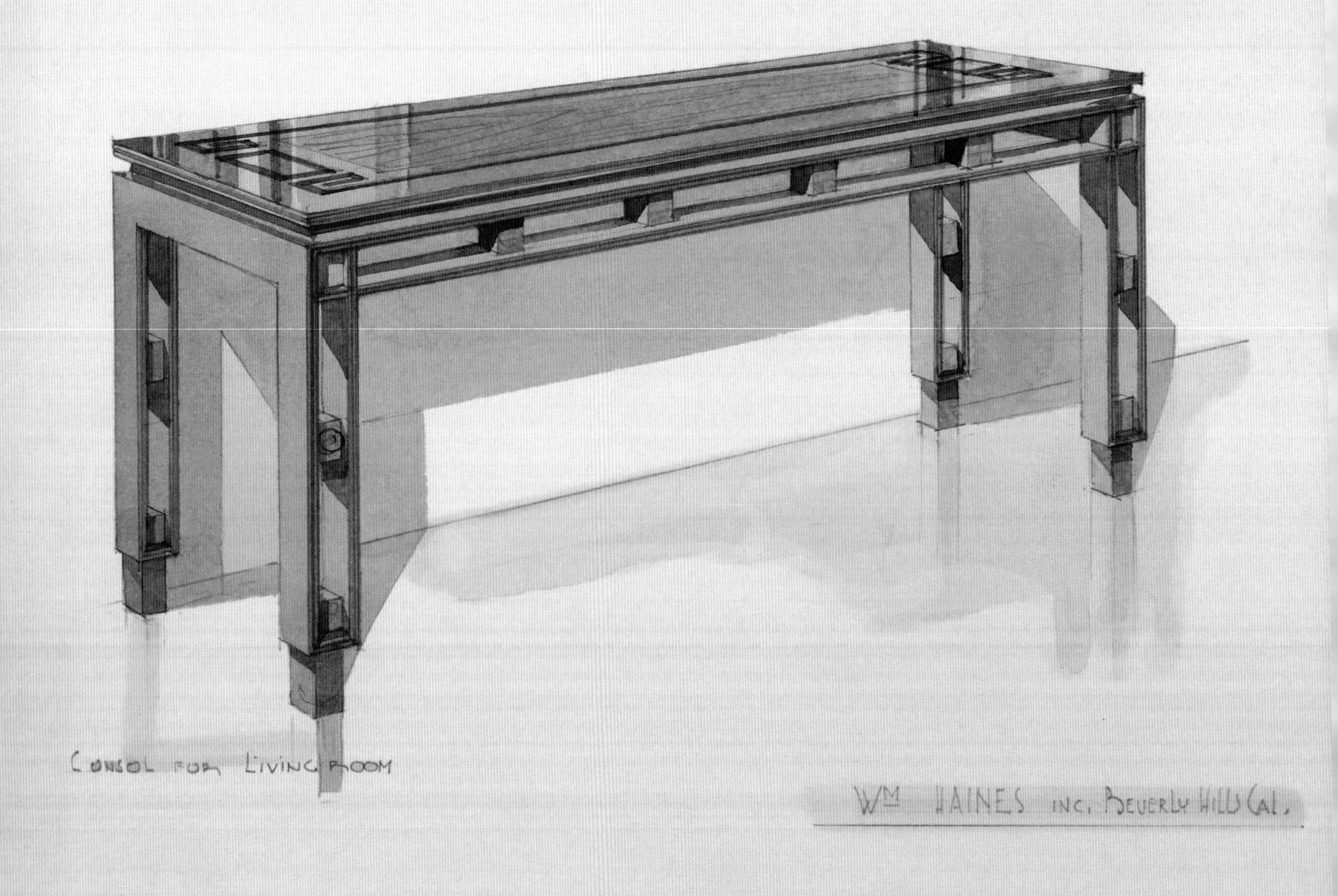

Above This console was never built for Sunnylands but was adapted as a backgammon table.

Opposite above The dining room sideboard. Peter Schifando, current owner of William Haines Designs, says, "The furniture is relatively quiet. The furnishings and the backgrounds that Haines did were very elegant and somewhat spare. They weren't meant to overpower."

Opposite below The watercolor for the proposed sideboard anticipates the importance of the Impressionist paintings within the furnishings scheme.

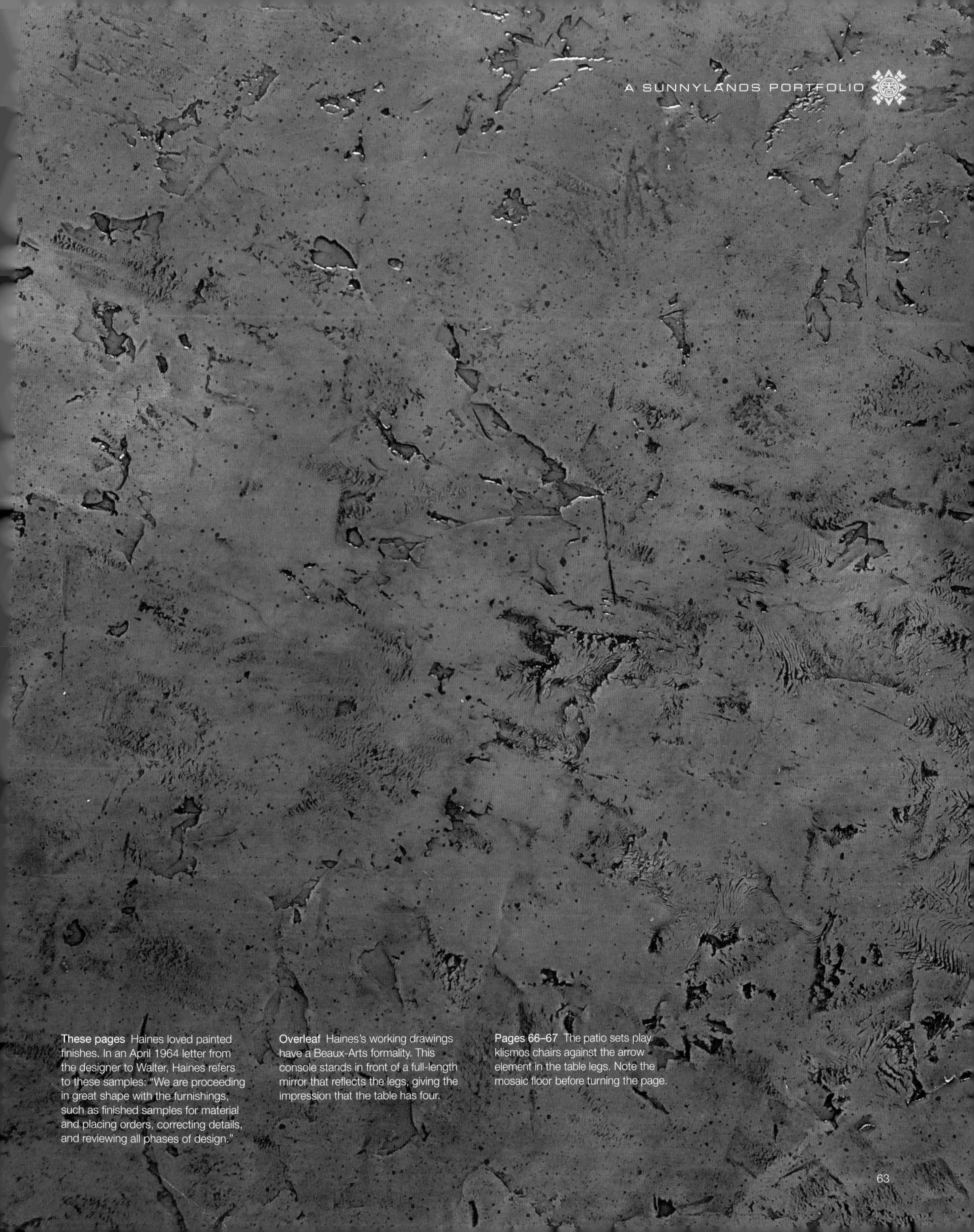

These pages Haines loved painted finishes. In an April 1964 letter from the designer to Walter, Haines refers to these samples: "We are proceeding in great shape with the furnishings, such as finished samples for material and placing orders, correcting details, and reviewing all phases of design."

Overleaf Haines's working drawings have a Beaux-Arts formality. This console stands in front of a full-length mirror that reflects the legs, giving the impression that the table has four.

Pages 66–67 The patio sets play klismos chairs against the arrow element in the table legs. Note the mosaic floor before turning the page.

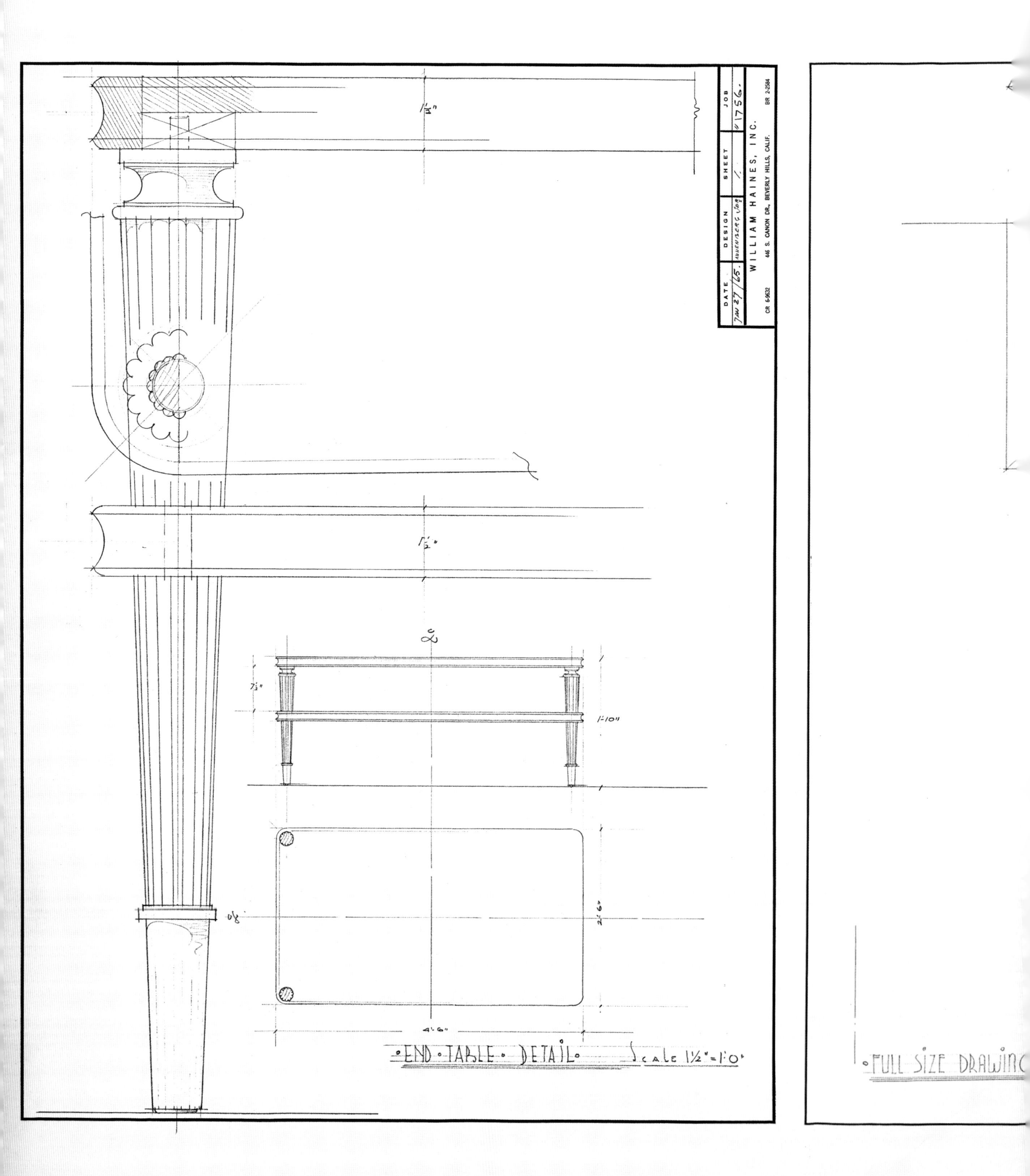

DATE
DESIGN
SHEET
JOB
JAN 27/65.
1756.
WILLIAM HAINES, INC.
CR 6-9632
446 S. CANON DR., BEVERLY HILLS, CALIF.
BR 2-2584
1'-10"
2'-6"
4'-6"
END TABLE DETAIL
SCALE 1½" = 1'0"
FULL SIZE

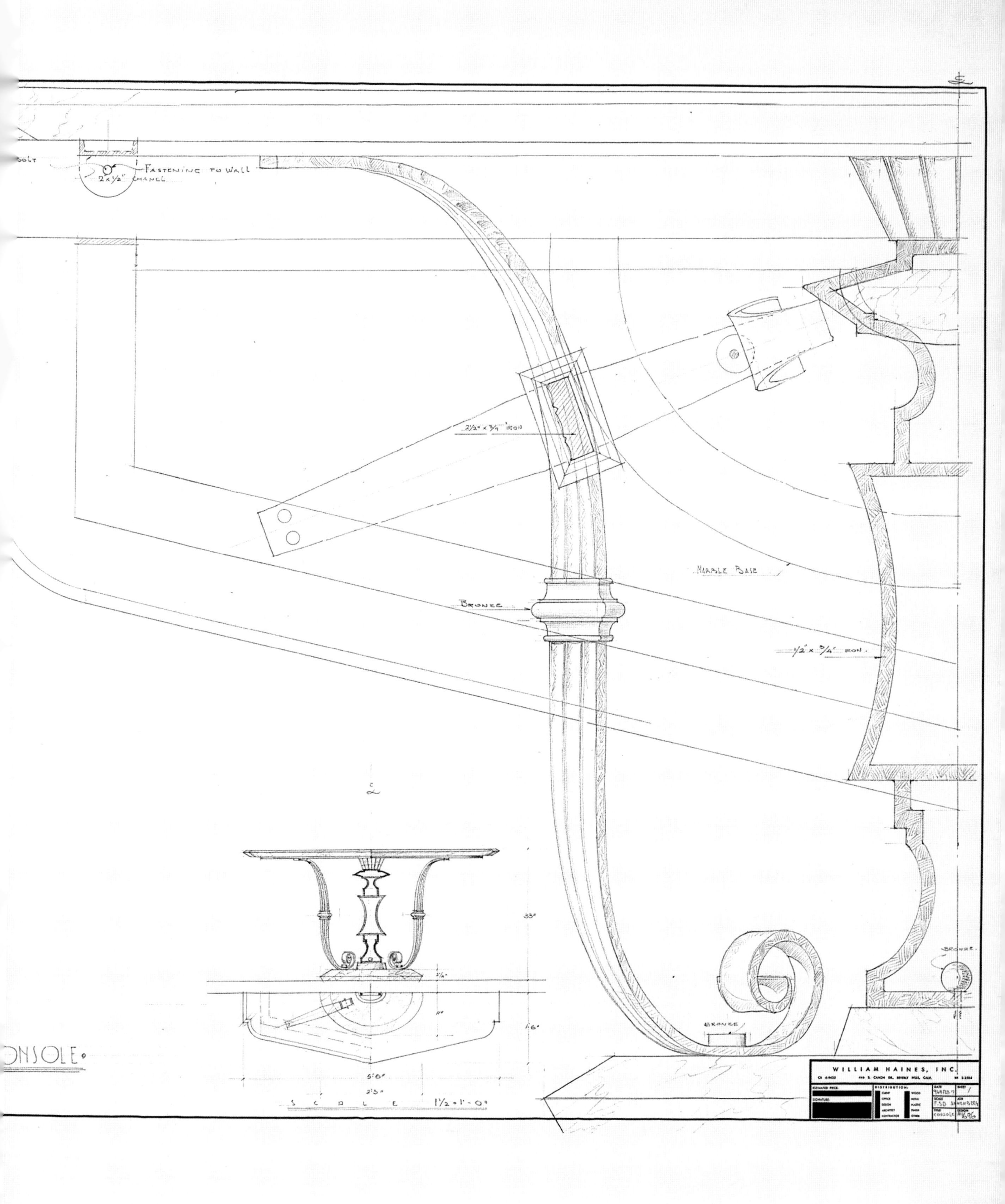
Fastening to Wall
2 x 1/2" chanel
2 1/2" x 3/4" iron
Marble Base
Bronze
1/2" x 3/4" iron
Bronze
Bronze
33"
1'-6"
5'-6"
2'-5"
ONSOLE
Scale 1 1/2 = 1'-0"
WILLIAM HAINES, INC.
446 S. Canon Dr., Beverly Hills, Calif.
Estimated Price:
Signature:
Distribution:
Client
Office
Design
Architect
Contractor
Wood
Metal
Plastic
Finish
Other
Date
Sheet 1
Scale
Job
Title Console
Design

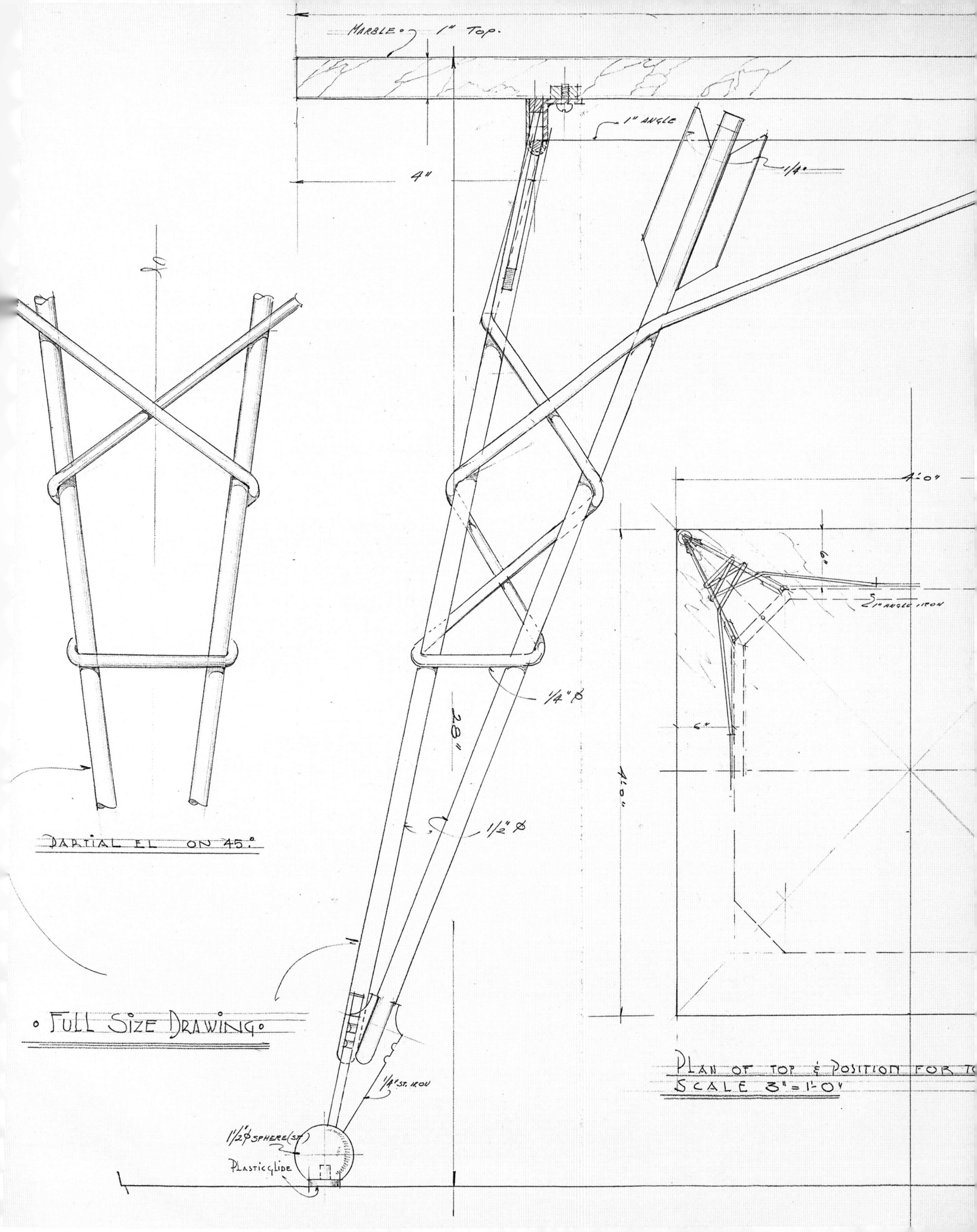

MARBLE 1" TOP.
1" ANGLE
1/4"
4"
PARTIAL EL ON 45°
1/4" Ø
28"
4'-0"
1/2" Ø
4'-0"
6"
2 1" ANGLE IRON
6"
• FULL SIZE DRAWING •
1/4" ST. IRON
1 1/2" Ø SPHERE (ST)
PLASTIC GLIDE
PLAN OF TOP & POSITION FOR TO
SCALE 3" = 1'-0"

·MOZAÌC · FLOOR'S·

·DESIGN · FOR LIVING TERRACE·

When Walter inquired about the possibility of buying an ancient mosaic for the terrace, William Haines designed a mosaic carpet using segments that were produced by the Frugoli Marble Company in Italy. Italian stone carvers supplied the cut stones and California stonemasons installed them.

• S C A L E 1" = 1' 0" •

SUNNYLANDS ROOM BY ROOM

While its architectural pedigree is impressive enough, Sunnylands has another distinction: it is the only extant preserved interior by William Haines, one of America's most celebrated designers, that is open to the public. A box-office star who appeared in silent films for Metro-Goldwyn-Mayer in the 1920s, William "Billy" Haines used his Hollywood contacts to start a design business in 1930. Working with actors such as Carole Lombard, Norma Shearer, and William Powell, as well as with the head of Warner Bros. Studios Jack Warner, Haines built up an impressive Hollywood clientele. In 1945, Ted Graber joined the firm and continued its work after Haines's death in 1973, selling the business in 1985 to Peter Schifando, who continues to operate William Haines Designs.

The Haines style featured European and Chinese antiques mixed with Haines-designed furnishings and abundant light—a significant shift from the dark Spanish Revival interiors that had been the rage in California in the 1920s.

According to Peter Schifando, "In every design project there's a color palette which gets developed. At Sunnylands, it was derived from the mountains, the desert, and the colors that were around. There's a great quiet in the desert, which is very nice, so you want to play to that." Unlike many fine examples of midcentury modernism in Palm Springs, where the architecture and interior both reflect an interest in new materials and functional shapes, Sunnylands' interiors are much more traditional than its architecture.

William Haines's interest in modern simple shapes did not extend to modern materials. Unlike designers Charles and Ray Eames, George Nelson, or Verner Panton, Haines celebrated fine fabrics and avoided any mass-produced material. He used custom fabrics with elaborate flat embroidery and trapunto quilting, which recalled the lushness of historic craftsmanship to communicate uniqueness. Haines designed every piece of furniture in the house—all of the sofas, tables, chairs, lamps, and mirrors—to capture a sense of luxury mixed with informality. The low profiles and elongated lines of these furnishings highlight the people gathered in the space. Jean Mathison, Haines's assistant on the project, described the design of the house as "soft modern."

Although the architecture at Sunnylands reflected a Mayan theme, that theme is not evident in the furnishings. William Haines wrote to Walter: "I feel it was Quincy's intent, and I most surely know it is mine, that your house should definitely be as timeless as it can be, or as much as Jones can make it, and I can furnish it." Sunnylands' interiors highlight the quiet richness of the furnishings, fine art, and decorative arts in relation to the simplified lines of the architecture and the organic quality of the landscape.

THE ENTRY COURT

The first room one enters at Sunnylands is actually an outdoor room with two walls of hedges and two lava-stone walls that form a square containing a circular driveway. At its center is the twenty-foot Mexican Column, covered with symbols of Aztec, Mayan, colonial, and contemporary Mexican history, that the Annenbergs commissioned from José and Tomás Chávez Morado as a smaller-scale version of the column the couple saw in 1967 at the Museo Nacional de Antropología in Mexico City.

THE ATRIUM AND LIVING ROOM

The front doors of the house open to a 6,500-square-foot room with an atrium containing a sunken planter of pink bromeliads within which stands Auguste Rodin's bronze sculpture, *Eve*. Positioning the front doors at a forty-five-degree angle provides a diagonal view into the space, making it seem even larger than it is.

When Leonore first saw the perforated steel columns that support the pyramidal roof and define the atrium, she was horrified. "We stood there aghast . . . we said we have a monster on our hands . . . it's the worst thing I'd ever seen." The Annenbergs worked with Jones to modify the design, leaving the steel exposed as Jones had wished, but painted in an agreeable color, with round pegs inserted in the holes to refine their appearance. The circular detail in these columns is repeated in the housing of the skylight.

The color scheme for much of the house—the atrium, living room, hallways, and dining room—is established here. The soft celadon green complements the rose marble floors and the views of various green trees and shrubs outside. The use of a very pale celadon fabric for the sofas in this

Page 70 The silk-and-linen fabric on this stool features trapunto quilting in a flower design. Stools are tucked under coffee tables throughout the house.

Page 71 This open-armed Seniah chair is one of a pair in this living room seating area. *Seniah* is Haines spelled backward.

Pages 72–73 Auguste Rodin's sculpture of *Eve* draws visitors into a light-filled space both during the day and in the evening.

space also allows the eye to travel from painting to painting, lamp to lamp, and Chinese Tang dynasty funerary figures to Chinese cloisonné objects.

William Haines had a genius for identifying objects that were visually appealing but could be adapted for functional use. Every lamp showcases Chinese ceramic or metal pieces, without damaging them, by employing a so-called museum mount.

The finest of the trapunto quilting can be seen in the living room, creating lattice and circular patterns in three dimensions on fabrics and allowing light and shadow to enhance the flat tops of the stools, sections of the side cushions, and the flat areas of sofas and chairs. The quilting is specific to each piece and its location, not part of an overall pattern that is then cut and used throughout the house. The sofas closest to the fireplace in the living room have the added element of elaborate floral embroidery.

Beginning in 1974, the Annenbergs' collection of paintings was placed throughout the house, with the largest and most impressive canvases in the atrium and living room. In 1983, the collection was expanded when Walter purchased fifteen major works from his sister Enid Haupt. Landscape paintings by Monet and Cézanne hung in the living room with van Gogh's *Roses* and Renoir's *The Daughters of Catulle Mendès*. Later acquisitions included Matisse's *Odalisque with Grey Trousers* and Picasso's *Au Lapin Agile*, which Walter purchased at auction in 1990. Showing nineteenth- and early twentieth-century paintings against rough, dark lava stone was unusual in the 1970s. At the time, art galleries typically had white walls and even traditional hanging was done against painted walls or wallpaper. As it turned out, the dark, rich lava stone was the perfect backdrop for the collection's vibrant colors.

Following Walter Annenberg's death in 2002, the paintings were transferred to the Metropolitan Museum of Art in New York permanently. The Met created digital reproductions for Leonore, who enjoyed these reminders of the collection for the last seven years of her life. Because the paintings are central to the experience of Sunnylands, the reproductions recreate the atmosphere of the house during its period of greatest historical significance.

The Annenbergs also collected twentieth-century modern sculptures, including two Auguste Rodins, an Alberto Giacometti, five Jean Arps, and works by Yaacov Agam, Harry Bertoia, and Émile Gilioli. Two large-scale female figures by Arp flank the front doors and Rodin's *Eve* takes center stage in the atrium. Rodin's *Eternal Spring* resided in the garden outside, directly adjacent to the living room. Giacometti's *Bust of Diego on Stele III* stood beside Pablo Picasso's *Au Lapin Agile*, and intimate Arp sculptures dotted the atrium/living room. This small but smart collection traces modern European sculpture from its beginnings with Rodin to the simplified forms of Arp, to the expressive surface texture of Giacometti, and to the use of movement by Bertoia and Agam.

The interior furnishings have remained relatively constant since 1966 with only a few exceptions. Originally, the living room sofas were placed on a diagonal, but that arrangement changed by the 1970s. Leonore's penchant for balance almost certainly drove the change to a more traditional placement of sofas with two chairs on a ninety-degree angle. The Annenbergs initially included area rugs in the living room but later removed them, emphasizing the beauty of the marble floor. When the formal dining room was finished in 1977, a new seating arrangement and shelves featuring signed photographs of British royalty replaced the original dining table in the living room—the newly furnished room was dubbed the Royal Sitting Room. All fabric changes were made by Haines and Graber, who also suggested decorative art objects, though the number of objects increased as Leonore added gifts to tables and shelves. She had a preference for symmetrical arrangements so pairs of objects—whether Chinese ceramics or cloisonné—were displayed, or the arrangement included a single vase flanked by two similar birds, flowers, or animals.

Overleaf More than three hundred pink-flowering bromeliads create the garden that surrounds *Eve*. Architect A. Quincy Jones designed the pivoting marble base for the sculpture in June 1965.

Right Lava stone walls increased the brilliance of the colors of the Impressionist and Post-Impressionist paintings in the atrium and living room.

Overleaf Vincent van Gogh's *Roses* hung above the fireplace, which was never lit. New research has revealed that these flowers were originally pink, but the use of a fugitive paint color rendered them white long before the Annenbergs purchased the painting.

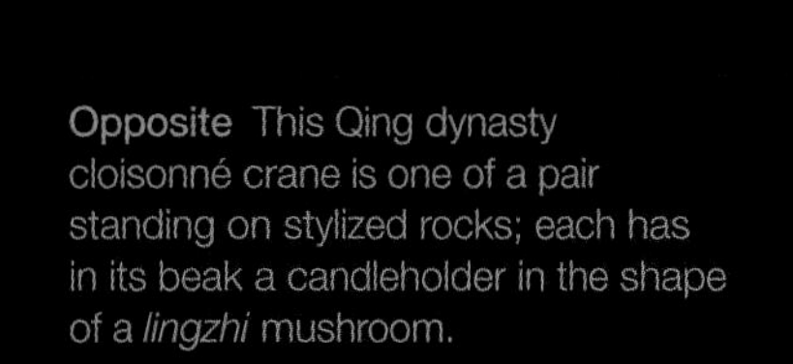

Opposite This Qing dynasty cloisonné crane is one of a pair standing on stylized rocks; each has in its beak a candleholder in the shape of a *lingzhi* mushroom.

Left The motif of the red bat, which symbolizes "blessings" or "happiness," is seen on a large *meiping* vase from the Qianlong period (1736–96) of the Qing dynasty.

Right A cloisonné incense burner in the shape of a bird, from the Qing dynasty (1644–1912) or Republic of China (1912–49).

Preceding pages Claude Monet's *Water Lilies* (1919) hangs on painted wood paneling above a sofa. Brickwork quilting on the chairs echoes the painted burlwood finish of the coffee table.

Below Extensive flat embroidery on the backs and seats of chairs and sofas was enhanced by trapunto quilting.

Opposite This hostess chair in celadon lacquer finish with seat and back upholstered in celadon silk canvas features a trapunto design on the seat.

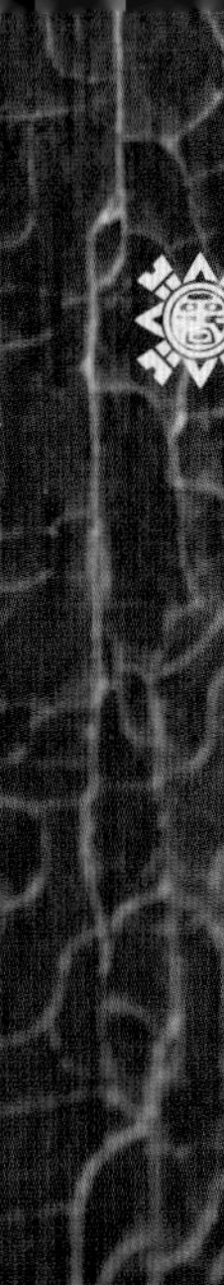

Above Beaded-metal doorknobs in the Calcutta style by Schlage were used throughout the house; they were sometimes painted to match doors.

Opposite Circular cutouts on the metal wings of the monitor cast light and shadows inside the atrium.

Right The bronze *Sculpture Classique* (1960) by Jean Arp is a modern contrast with Auguste Rodin's *Eve* as a welcome at the front door.

Overleaf Tang dynasty funerary earthenware pieces with three-color (*sancai*) glaze are displayed on a table adjacent to the atrium.

Pages 94–95 Six klismos chairs covered in celadon kidskin surround a six-sided inlaid table with Haines's signature pedestal base.

Opposite A pair of gold-mounted rock crystal giraffes by the Parisian firm Boucheron adorn the hexagonal table in the living room.

Above A *famille verte* biscuit sweetmeat dish, from the Kangxi period (1662–1722) of the Qing dynasty.

Overleaf left Two klismos-style chairs with turquoise leather seats and walnut frames match the backgammon board where the Annenbergs played regularly.

Overleaf right "The vigorous movement of the colors, the bold forms, reminded me so much of van Gogh," Walter said of this Ming dynasty (1368–1644) cloisonné panel (detail shown).

Opposite Étienne Hajdú's keen eye for selecting marble as well as his skill as a carver are evident in *Belle de Nuit 1958*.

Right *The Unicorn* crystal piece was derived from a drawing by Pakistani artist Sheikh Ahmed and created by Steuben designer George Thompson as part of the *Asian Artists in Crystal* series.

Below This massive twentieth-century pale green jadeite figure of a recumbent water buffalo was sometimes referred to as "Walter."

Right A view of the crystal objects exhibited in the Steuben Gallery outside the dining room. The Annenbergs owned many Steuben pieces, including works from the *Great Explorer*, *Islands in Crystal*, *Poetry in Crystal*, and *Masterworks* series, as well as the only complete set of *Asian Artists in Crystal*.

Top A giant rising with the sun along the Nile is the centerpiece of this Steuben crystal object designed by Lloyd Atkins, based on a drawing by Egyptian Gamal Sagini, for the *Asian Artists in Crystal* series.

Above Also part of the *Asian Artists* series, *The Village of Malinao*, based on a drawing by Filipino artist Manuel Rodriguez, depicts a succession of village scenes.

THE DINING ROOM

Opposite Georg Jensen silver centerpieces are complemented by Boehm *Lee Annenberg* pink roses in this luncheon setting on the ivory inlaid table.

Overleaf This table setting features vermeil flatware and Flora Danica china, made by the Royal Copenhagen porcelain manufactory after 1922.

Pages 108–9 A silver tureen and a pair of candelabra designed by Danish silversmith Georg Jensen adorn the sideboard in the dining room.

The formal dining room is approached through the Steuben Gallery. In 1971, Walter purchased the *Asian Artists in Crystal* series from Steuben Glass—the only complete example of the series. The thirty-six pieces were part of a diplomatic exchange conducted during Dwight Eisenhower's presidency. First exhibited at the National Gallery of Art in Washington, D.C., in January 1956, the series was then shown at the Metropolitan Museum of Art in New York in February/March and subsequently toured sixteen countries. Drawings collected from Asian artists inspired the creation of objects made and engraved by American craftsmen. This collaboration was of special interest to Walter and Leonore because both believed in the importance of cultural diplomacy.

The two round mahogany and ivory-inlaid tables were designed by William Haines. Customarily, twelve people were seated at the large table and ten at the smaller one. The Annenbergs split up at dinner—each one the host of a table. Couples were often seated separately, too, to create the best dynamic for conversation.

The dining room also features the collection of Georg Jensen silver that Moses Annenberg bought for his wife in 1935–36. Georgian, Regency, and Victorian silver-gilt pieces often decorated the dining tables. The large painting called *The Album* by Édouard Vuillard was a special favorite because seven women can be seen in the work, reminding Walter of his seven sisters. The *Blanc de Chine* or Dehua sculpture of Guanyin, the Goddess of Mercy, stands sentinel. Views out the window focus on Harry Bertoia's *Peacock*—a kinetic piece that moves gently in the breeze.

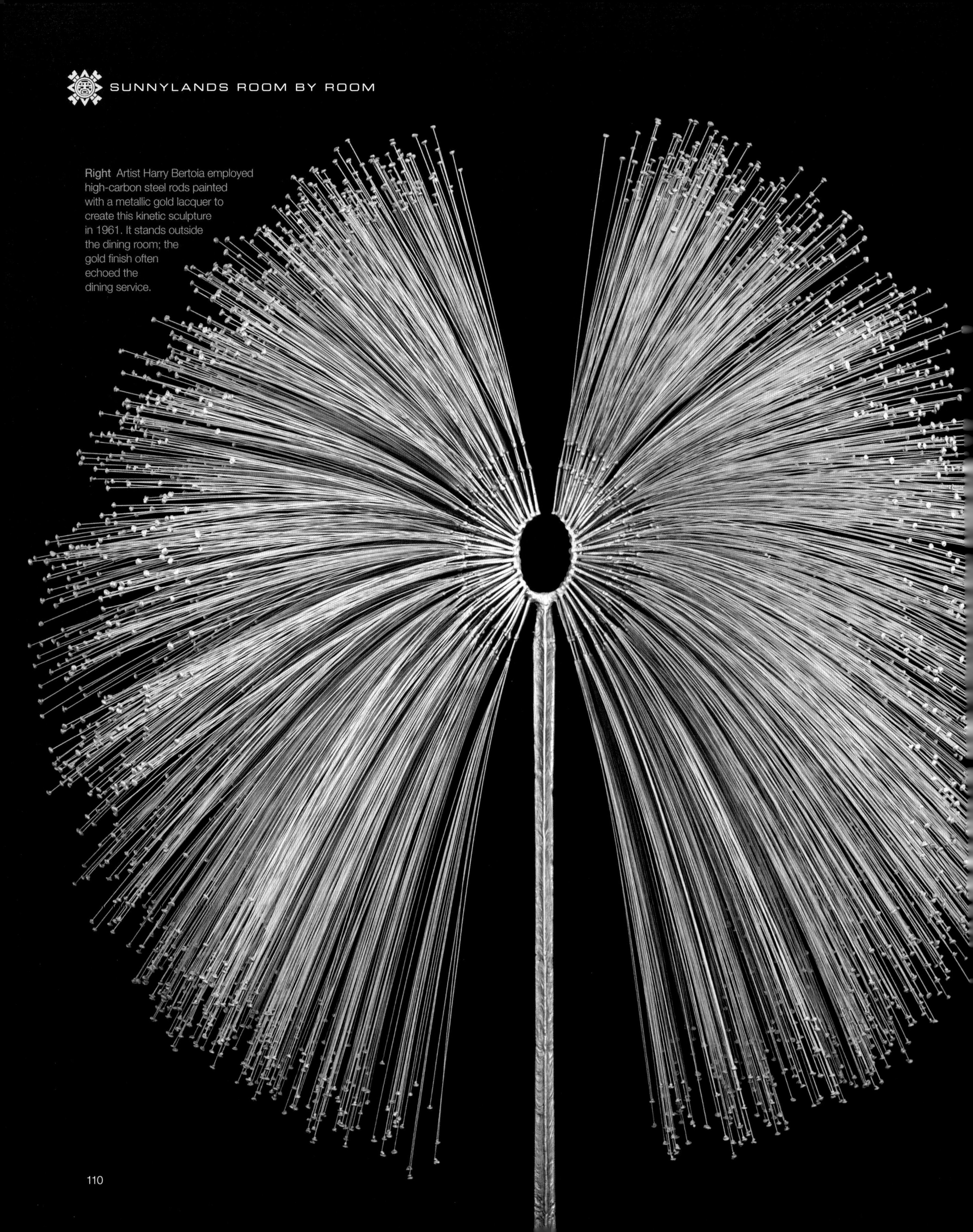

Right Artist Harry Bertoia employed high-carbon steel rods painted with a metallic gold lacquer to create this kinetic sculpture in 1961. It stands outside the dining room; the gold finish often echoed the dining service.

Above left This shrine in the shape of a pagoda could have been commissioned for a temple or as part of a private altar during the middle to late Qing dynasty (1644–1912). The Loyal General, one of the Seven Treasures, is depicted kneeling and brandishing a sword on a platform in the shape of a lotus flower.

Above right The *Chinese Pavilion*, from the Steuben *Masterworks* series, was designed by Donald Pollard in 1974 incorporating gold, jade, and jewel-mounted crystal. The Annenbergs owned four of the nine *Masterworks* created by Steuben.

Right A detail of a silver-gilt epergne made by Thomas Pitts in London in 1761–62. The Annenbergs often used it as a dining table centerpiece, filled with flowers or sweets.

THE ROOM OF MEMORIES

Originally designed as a guest room for Walter's mother, who died before the house was completed, this room was redesigned by Harry Saunders in 1977 as an informal library with bookshelves. Saunders enlarged the room by claiming the original garden patio space and adding a skylight. The room provided the perfect setting for a growing collection of rare and autographed books and for the display of photographs, correspondence, awards, and memorabilia, which tell the story of the Annenberg family. These photographs include documentation of Queen Elizabeth II's visit to Sunnylands in 1983, the Christmas cards sent by Elizabeth the Queen Mother from 1972 to 2001, the annual New Year's Eve parties, and presidential connections over the decades.

A family wall tells the photographic story of Walter's grandparents, parents, and children. An unusual panoramic view shows the staff at Triangle Publications, Inc. when Moses was chairman. A photo of President Ronald Reagan in this very room, watching Soviet leader Mikhail Gorbachev deliver a speech on nuclear disarmament to the American people, reflects the level of historical events that took place at Sunnylands.

Rembrandt Peale's 1859 *Portrait of George Washington* is arresting, but it is Andrew Wyeth's 1978 portrait of Walter Annenberg that commands attention in this room. Walter's belief that the greatest thing a man can do is serve his country is reflected in the pairing of these two paintings and the messages contained in so many of the items featured in the Room of Memories.

Opposite The Room of Memories is known for its coral scheme, its skylights, and an extraordinary collection of photographs and memorabilia.

Overleaf Ronald Reagan gave his final radio address as president during this New Year's stay at Sunnylands.

WA

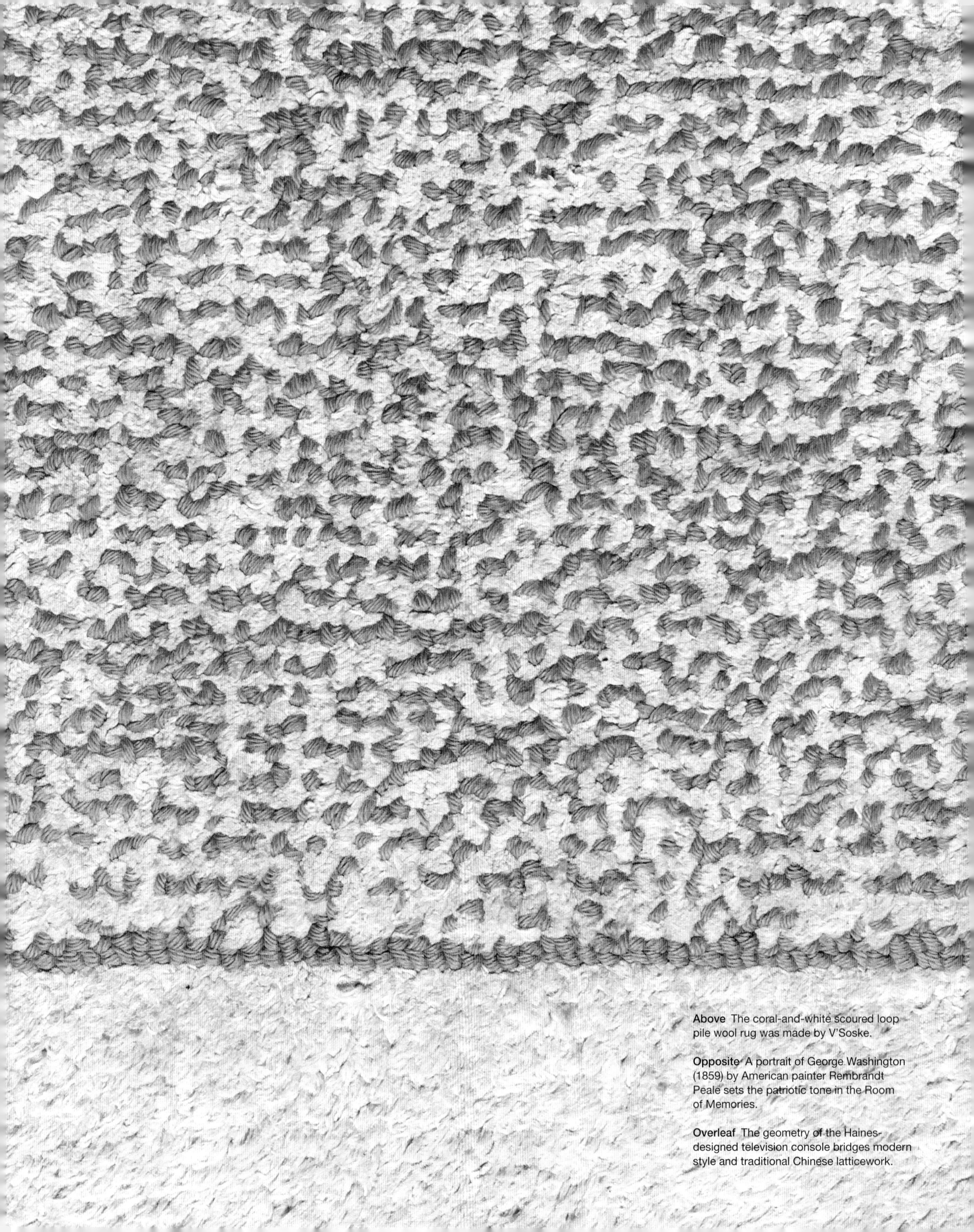

Above The coral-and-white scoured loop pile wool rug was made by V'Soske.

Opposite A portrait of George Washington (1859) by American painter Rembrandt Peale sets the patriotic tone in the Room of Memories.

Overleaf The geometry of the Haines-designed television console bridges modern style and traditional Chinese latticework.

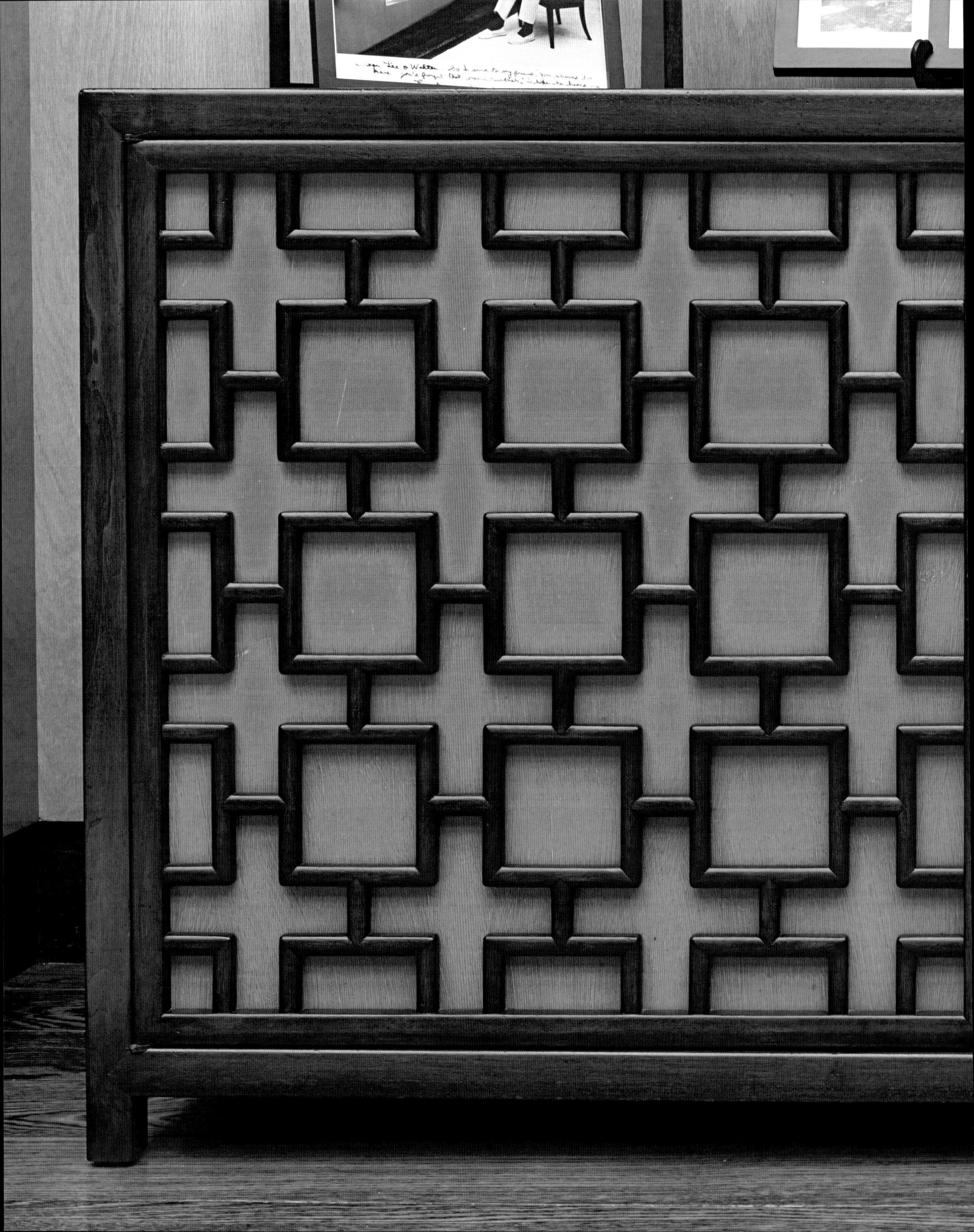

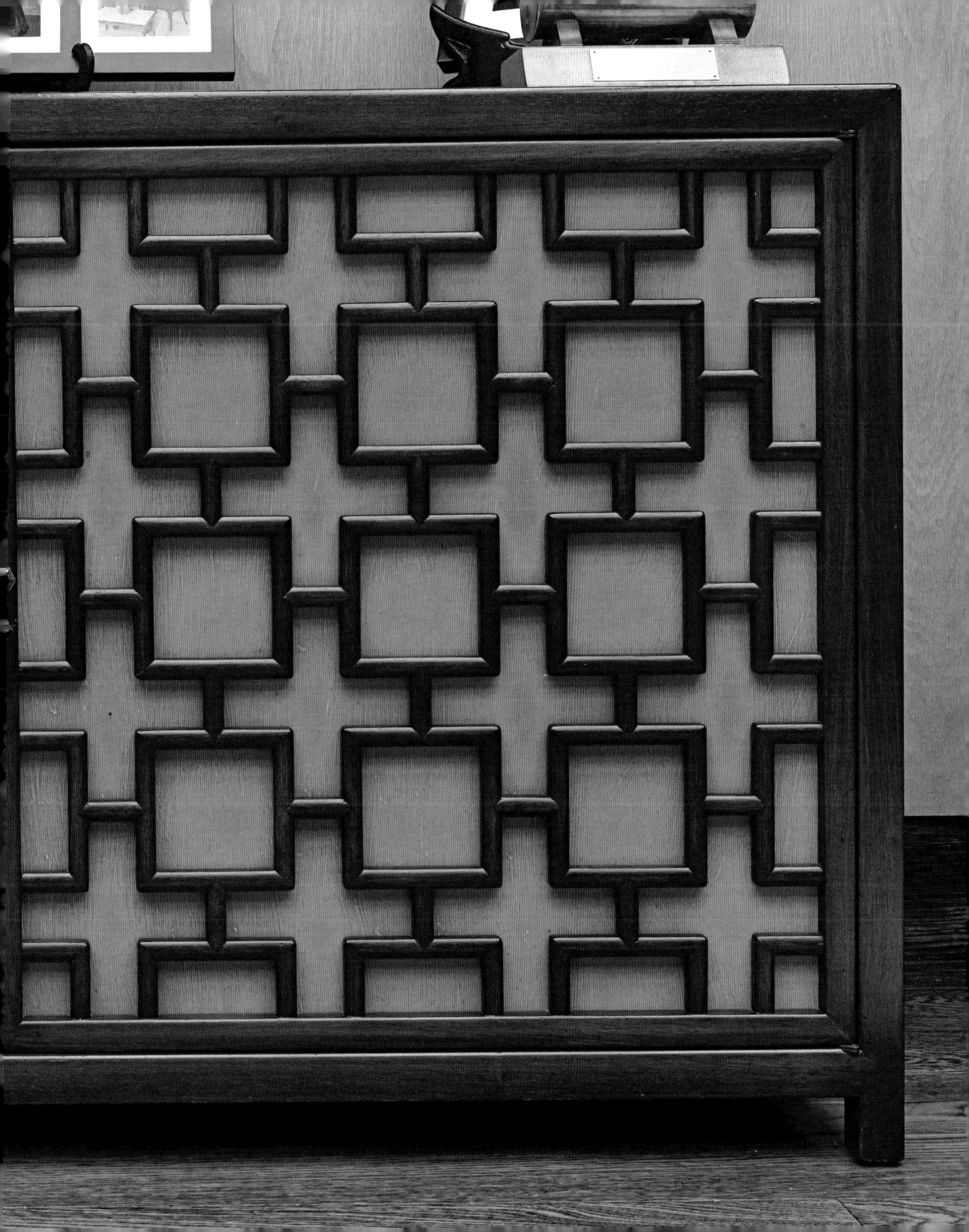

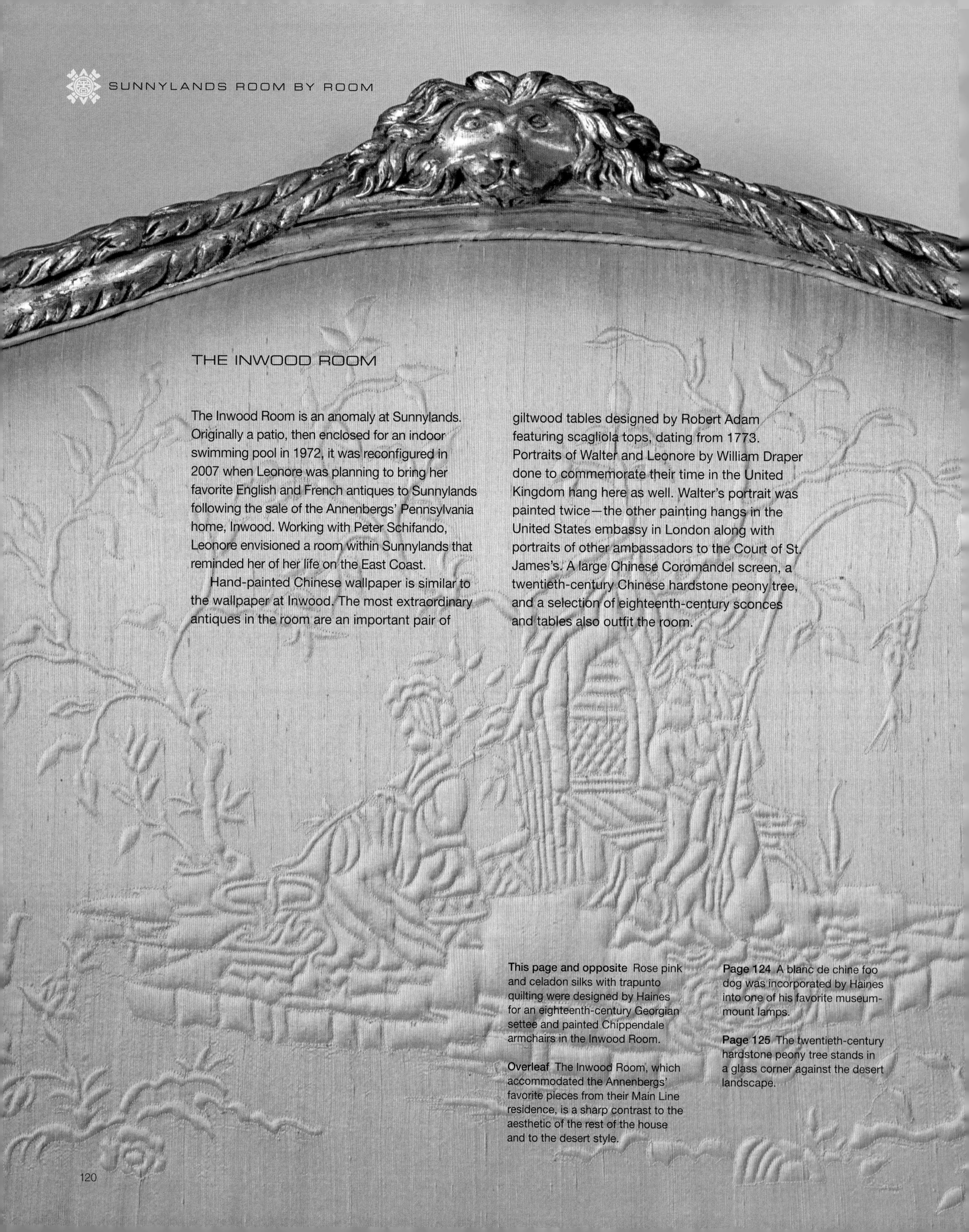

THE INWOOD ROOM

The Inwood Room is an anomaly at Sunnylands. Originally a patio, then enclosed for an indoor swimming pool in 1972, it was reconfigured in 2007 when Leonore was planning to bring her favorite English and French antiques to Sunnylands following the sale of the Annenbergs' Pennsylvania home, Inwood. Working with Peter Schifando, Leonore envisioned a room within Sunnylands that reminded her of her life on the East Coast.

Hand-painted Chinese wallpaper is similar to the wallpaper at Inwood. The most extraordinary antiques in the room are an important pair of giltwood tables designed by Robert Adam featuring scagliola tops, dating from 1773. Portraits of Walter and Leonore by William Draper done to commemorate their time in the United Kingdom hang here as well. Walter's portrait was painted twice—the other painting hangs in the United States embassy in London along with portraits of other ambassadors to the Court of St. James's. A large Chinese Coromandel screen, a twentieth-century Chinese hardstone peony tree, and a selection of eighteenth-century sconces and tables also outfit the room.

This page and opposite Rose pink and celadon silks with trapunto quilting were designed by Haines for an eighteenth-century Georgian settee and painted Chippendale armchairs in the Inwood Room.

Overleaf The Inwood Room, which accommodated the Annenbergs' favorite pieces from their Main Line residence, is a sharp contrast to the aesthetic of the rest of the house and to the desert style.

Page 124 A blanc de chine foo dog was incorporated by Haines into one of his favorite museum-mount lamps.

Page 125 The twentieth-century hardstone peony tree stands in a glass corner against the desert landscape.

CLASSIC ACT
VAN GOGH A RETROSPECTIVE

THE MASTER BEDROOM

While Walter was alive, this room had a significant amount of rust-colored fabric on faux oak finish chairs. Following Walter's death, Leonore worked with Peter Schifando, who had purchased William Haines Designs, to design a bedroom that was more purely feminine. A four-poster queen-size bed was introduced and the chairs were refinished with an ivory surface and covered with yellow fabrics.

This room, with its yellow carpet and yellow curtains, is balanced by the view of the cactus garden and the sweeping views of one of the estate's eleven lakes and a rolling lawn dotted with mature trees. One of the most striking pieces in the house is the modern Recamier sofa with Haines's trademark biscuit tufting and leather-wrapped legs.

Haines designed the bedside tables to swing the shelf toward or away from the bed. Leonore's collection of Battersea boxes includes many gifts from friends and family over the years. Currently this room reflects elements of Leonore's changes as well as the reintroduction of a king-size bed with a very low profile, which was how the room looked when the couple shared the space.

Opposite In 2007, Leonore lightened the bedroom furnishings scheme and had this tub chair refinished and reupholstered by Peter Schifando of William Haines Designs.

Above An exuberant ribbon pull on a bedside table.

Overleaf William Haines described the eight-foot sofa in his inventory of furnishings as "specially designed," with an "off-white silk texture, self welts and buttons, exposed metal frame wrapped in white leather."

Pages 130–31 A close look at the "unicorn" leather-wrapped frame and biscuit tufting.

Pages 132–33 Rotating bedside tables were a favorite Haines device. Jacques Villon's *L'Enfant au Biberon* (1952) hangs against *faux bois* paneling.

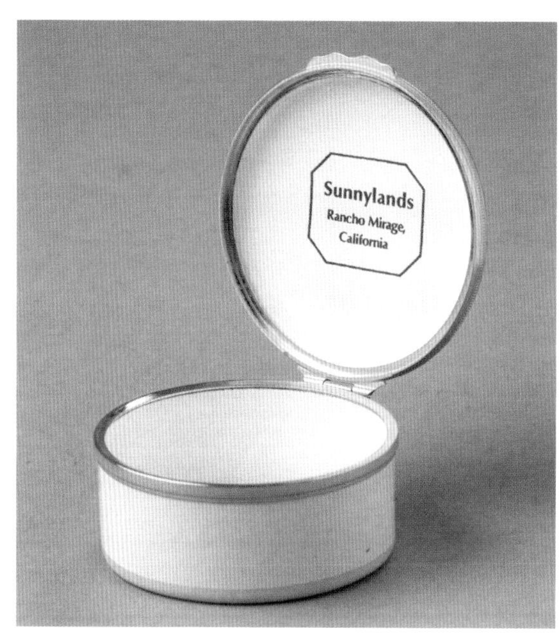

Left Given as a hostess gift at the New Year's Eve party in 1980, this enamel box with the Sunnylands emblem was produced by Halcyon Days in London.

Below Chinese famille rose, peacock pattern, and armorial export porcelain chargers and a pair of *meiping*-shaped yellow glazed jars populate the shelves above Leonore's desk. Two ceramic European parrots resting on green rocks (c. 1785) are mounted as the lamp base.

Opposite This detail highlights the exquisite colors and relief of the Chinese yellow-ground porcelain vase with the "hundred antiques motif" that was mounted as a lamp in the master bedroom.

Overleaf Leonore's sunken marble bathtub has gold-plated Sherle Wagner fittings.

壽

THE GUEST WING

The original guest wing had two bedroom suites with a shared space called the Game Room, which features an entirely different sensibility from the main house. The elegant tones of celadon and pink give way to vibrant yellow sunflowers and yellow lacquered chairs arranged around red leather–covered card tables. A wall of sunflower curtains faces a wall of walnut cabinets that provide space for sunflower-design serving pieces. Hidden behind those cabinets is a projection room that houses two 35mm projectors used for showing the first-run films that the Annenbergs arranged. Sometimes those movies were shared with neighbor Frank Sinatra—one night the projectionist ran the movie at Sunnylands, and the next night he showed it at Sinatra's compound. Movie nights included potato chips, popcorn, and other snacks, arranged neatly in vertical rows within Plexiglas containers.

The two original guest suites were called the Pink Room and the Yellow Room. The choice of a scattered rose pattern for the quilted fabric on the headboards, sofas, upholstered chairs, and bed skirts was complemented by striped curtains and fabric on the walls. Faux finishes in the appropriate color enhanced the wooden desks, tables, and chairs. Botanical prints were sandwiched between sheets of glass in pink or yellow frames. Even the jelly beans were color coordinated. The 1977 expansion of the guest quarters added three rooms in three additional colors: peach, blue, and green.

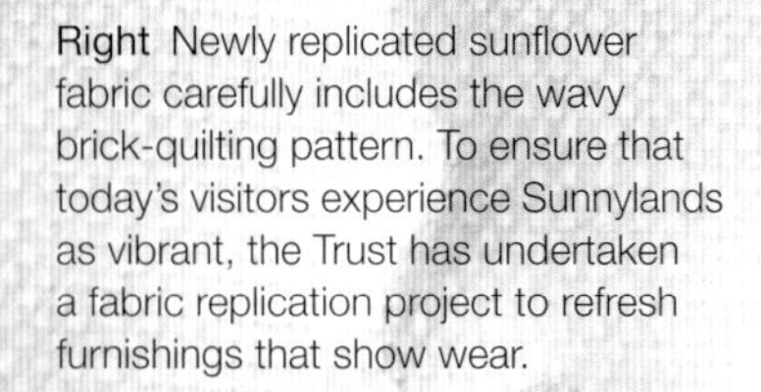

Right Newly replicated sunflower fabric carefully includes the wavy brick-quilting pattern. To ensure that today's visitors experience Sunnylands as vibrant, the Trust has undertaken a fabric replication project to refresh furnishings that show wear.

Overleaf The Game Room, at the heart of the guest wing, was a place for lunches, relaxing, and watching movies during weekend stays.

Yourself

The Game Room cupboard was filled with sunflower-themed glasses, cups, and Fitz and Floyd salt and pepper shakers, along with yellow-and-white Thomas Goode tea sets.

Left The sunken bar in the Game Room was very much of the period. An Audubon Havell edition bird print and a hand-painted document that cites the land ownership history of the Sunnylands estate are among the decorations.

Above Massive 35mm projectors showed first-run movies to Annenberg guests.

Below Four bamboo-style chairs in yellow lacquer and leather surround a red leather card table with ebony legs.

Above This dark-stained oak tub chair was designed by Ted Graber, William Haines's associate and successor.

Opposite Two Prince Charles investiture chairs, designed in 1969 by Lord Snowdon, stand in the Game Room. The ash laminate is painted red and gilded with the Prince of Wales's feathers and his motto, *Ich Dien* (I Serve).

Overleaf Sunflower napkin rings were often used for lunches in the Game Room.

ICH
DIEN

Opposite Each guest room is known by its color. A pink scattered rose pattern on cotton established the palette for the Pink Room, which has welcomed Prince Andrew, David Rockefeller, Barbara Walters, Diane Sawyer, and Mike Nichols, among others.

Above Today's retreat participants often stay in the historic Pink Room, one of the original guest suites.

Left The midcentury chest of drawers has a painted finish in varying shades of pink.

Right Both Haines and the Annenbergs liked consistency and had the confidence to reuse a theme that served them well. Here, a chest of drawers in varying shades of yellow.

Below The Yellow Room was the favorite of the Reagans. Other occupants included Colin and Alma Powell, Princess Margaret, Steve Forbes, Henry Kissinger, and Hillary Clinton.

Opposite The scattered rose pattern in yellow is part of the current fabric replication project.

The Green Room was George H. W. Bush's favorite suite. It was closest to the lake and allowed quick access to morning fishing.

TRANSFORMING THE DESERT

Opposite The Eisenhower Palms mark the second fairway in this aerial view of the elevated green, ringed by bunkers.

In 1974, Walter Annenberg wrote to President Gerald Ford about the sanctuary aspect of Sunnylands: "The ancient Chinese philosophers believed that reverence of the landscape was the highest ideal in life and hence most Chinese paintings majored in some aspect of the landscape. Further, the landscape represented a sanctuary of protection and peaceful comfort. Sunnylands has come to represent just this in my life and as a consequence I try to guard the privacy and the beauty of it with respect and consideration."

To create this sanctuary, the design team needed to completely transform hundreds of acres of undeveloped desert, with its creosote bushes and blow sand. Architect A. Quincy Jones prepared the original site plan, which included a series of diagonal hedgerows throughout the property, creating a very angular layout. Renowned landscape architect Emmet Wemple was involved at this early stage of the design but withdrew as the project progressed. Whether it was in response to the realities of wind direction, the moving sand dunes, or the intensity of the heat, the design softened and tree plans changed from November 1964 to March 1965, with Jones submitting newer plans that showed tree bosques rather than hedgerows.

The details of planting were delegated to horticulturist Rolla Wilhite, who had a challenging job balancing the Annenbergs' desire for a green oasis with the realities

of the climate. Walter often suggested a possible plant for inclusion, and Wilhite then took him to various sites to explain the special treatment needed to sustain the plant in the desert. Required to replace dead trees under his contract—almost all of the 129 olive trees planted in September 1964 died in the first year—Wilhite recognized the critical timing for planting. Only trees planted from November to February were able to survive the grueling heat of the summer months. A team of thirty people worked on the job at the peak of the project. In the end, more than 6,000 trees were planted, largely eucalyptus, olive, tamarisk, oleander, carob, and oak.

Specimen trees are a big part of the story. In 1965, Wilhite purchased two 150-year-old Beaucarnea trees from the estate of Edward L. Doheny. Walter wanted to buy both of them but Wilhite would only sell one to the Annenbergs. It was moved to the desert on a flatbed truck at night over many days because of its size and impact on the roads. The glorious specimen was planted near the swimming pool and could be seen from all the rooms that faced west. It died in 2008, and a new tree with the same shape, though only seventy-five years old, has been planted to recreate the historic sightlines from the interior to the terrace.

Other specialty trees are the Eisenhower Palms suggested by former President Dwight Eisenhower in 1966 and the Nixon Magnolia given by President Richard Nixon in 1972. The cutting for the Nixon Magnolia came from the White House magnolia planted in the 1830s by President Andrew Jackson, which was from a tree at his Tennessee home, the Hermitage.

Wilhite also designed a cactus garden adjacent to the master bedroom, a garden area of dwarf Meyer lemon and evergreen pear trees near the dressing areas of the master bedroom, and the formal rose garden near the guest pavilion.

The elaborate irrigation system relied on wells that pumped water into a large lake, which served as a reservoir, along with twelve other lakes and connecting streams. Eleven lakes remain. These water features were integrated into the golf course design and introduced blue into the emerald green color scheme. The lakes also satisfied Walter's interest in birds, as they attracted resident and migratory birds in great numbers, providing a stopping point on the Pacific Flyway. Jones designed the organic-shaped swimming pool so that it was visually connected to the lakes, wanting the natural quality of the landscape to contrast with the strict geometry of the house.

The early years at Sunnylands best demonstrated the professionally designed landscape—a collaborative vision of designer and client. But from the 1970s on, additions and modifications augmented and altered that original vision, sometimes in significant ways. Preservation of the landscape today relies on the original design characteristics: a sense of enclosure; the theatrically choreographed arrival sequence; a distinction between "upstairs" and "downstairs"; the feeling of an oasis; and the midcentury concept of the blurring of indoors and outdoors.

The nine-hole golf course—each hole can be played two ways—was designed by Dick Wilson, a leading American golf course architect, with his associate Joe Lee. Wilson's signature style included elevated greens surrounded by bunkers or water. Hired by the Annenbergs in the fall of 1963, Wilson submitted his first golf course plans in early January 1964. He died in July 1965, about the time of the completion of the Annenberg course.

By 1982, Wilson's golf course was reportedly one of only two private courses in the United States, the other being one at the Rockefeller estate in Pocantico Hills. According to the book, *100 Greatest Golf Courses—And Then Some*, the one at Sunnylands was probably the country's "best-maintained golf course, over which the least number of rounds are played anywhere." Despite the limited number of golfers, the list is impressive. Presidents Dwight Eisenhower, Richard Nixon, Gerald Ford, Ronald Reagan, and George H. W. Bush, as well as Vice President Dan Quayle, have played the parkland course. Sports icons like Raymond Floyd, Arnold Palmer, Lee Trevino, and Tom Watson also have played, often in mixed groups of Annenberg friends, celebrities, and political figures. President Barack Obama has shared previous presidents' love of the course, playing golf at Sunnylands on six occasions between 2013 and 2016.

The Annenbergs played golf almost every day. Following the close of the stock market on the East Coast, Walter and Leonore went out for nine, eighteen, or twenty-seven holes. A maintenance worker followed behind and switched the pin placements to vary the experience for them. Leonore played more golf than Walter, and especially enjoyed her ladies' golf days,

An early aerial view of Sunnylands shows the location of the house and its oasis of green in yet-to-be-developed Rancho Mirage.

followed by lunch in the pink Chinese Pavilion on the course.

In 1968, a twenty-foot-tall Mexican column fountain by José and Tómas Chávez Morado was introduced into the entry court. Other exterior sculptures and follies dot the landscape, beginning with *Birds of Welcome* by Canadian artist Art Price installed in August 1971, Harry Bertoia's *Peacock* placed outside the dining room in 1974, Yaacov Agam's *Square Waves* installed adjacent to the pool in January 1976, the Kwakwaka'wakw totem pole by Canadian First Nations woodcarver Henry Hunt raised in 1976, the Chinese Pavilion constructed in 1976, and the Delos Bench delivered in 1979.

The most significant change to the estate boundary occurred in 1995, when the oleander bushes that enclosed the estate on two sides died in a desert-wide blight and were replaced by a pink wall. In 2001, an open pavilion designed by Palm Desert architect Alfred H. Cook was constructed as a mausoleum for both Walter and Leonore Annenberg within a private fifty-acre cemetery on the site. Special permission was granted for the interment of both Annenbergs on the estate.

The challenge today is how to balance historic preservation with retreat and public needs while being responsible stewards of more limited water resources. From 2010 to 2012, a restoration/renovation plan sought to return the golf course, as well as the planted areas around the house, to the original design intent. The scale of the trees, their health and their lifespans, as well as weather conditions, have been factors in changes over the years. From the outset, architect Jones questioned the use of Virginia Live Oak trees between the house and the outdoor trellises. Those fast-growing trees began to encroach on the pink roof by the 1980s and the Annenberg solution was to have them shaped into cylindrical topiaries. When the Trust inherited the property, the fifty-year-old trees, having outgrown their location, were removed and replaced with the same species, but are now maintained to control growth and keep their natural shape.

Grapefruit trees featured in the entry court died in 1982 due to a heavy frost; they were replaced by ficus trees but have now been replanted. In 1998, the rose garden was replanted with help from John N. Vogley Associates Landscape Architects to accommodate the Annenbergs' interest in signature roses—changing the design from bands of white, pink, and yellow to a mixed color palette with specialty roses like "Barbara Bush" and "Nancy Reagan."

To respond responsibly to the water shortage in California, a goal of a 50 percent reduction in water use was established in 2009 and has led to many upgrades. The remaining eleven lakes were relined, and a state-of-the-art irrigation system allows for more targeted delivery of water. Sixty acres of the original 180 acres of turf have been removed from irrigation; mulch and tall grass are now used beneath tree canopies and on the perimeter of the estate. The Annenbergs' annual water use was most intense during the five months a year that they stayed on the property. The Trust operates the site for public visitation and retreats on a nine-month schedule. As a result, the Trust has not yet achieved its 50 percent goal but continues to experiment with limited over-seeding and turf reduction.

Opposite This 2012 aerial view shows sixty acres of turf removed and replaced with mulch and non-irrigated tall grass around the perimeter and under tree canopies. The Sunnylands Center & Gardens, with its arid-landscape plants, is seen at the lower right.

Overleaf The pink-and-yellow color scheme extended to outdoor planting, as seen in the flowers blooming around the waterfall.

Above More than six hundred olive trees dot the landscape. The first Post-Impressionist painting purchased by the Annenbergs was Vincent van Gogh's *Olive Trees*; Walter loved the silvery color of the leaves. The Trust now harvests the olives and produces Sunnylands Olive Oil.

Opposite Reflections of large trees can be seen in several lakes. These bodies of water, so rare in the desert, offer watering stops for migrating birds.

Below The cactus garden off the master bedroom was the only example of arid-landscape planting on the historic estate.

Overleaf A view outside Walter's study. In February 1964, Walter wrote to A. Quincy Jones, "We might even have elements of cacti worked in on the golf course area."

Pages 170–171 William Haines designed furnishings like this green outdoor table as part of a suite of furniture complementing the geometries of the house.

Left The lines of the steel trellises and squares of the cement blocks were softened by cascading bougainvillea, which added color and informality to the bermed wall near the house.

Overleaf Desert light is not always sharp and harsh. This image captures a glimpse of the soft light that sometimes bathes the estate. A replacement Beaucarnea tree, only seventy-five years old, was planted in 2011 to reintroduce the original view from inside and around the house.

WESTERN

Preceding pages Leonore was still enjoying golf on her private course at age eighty-four, when this photograph was taken.

Right One of the initial plans for the golf course, presented by designer Dick Wilson in 1964, shows a nine-hole, par 36 course.

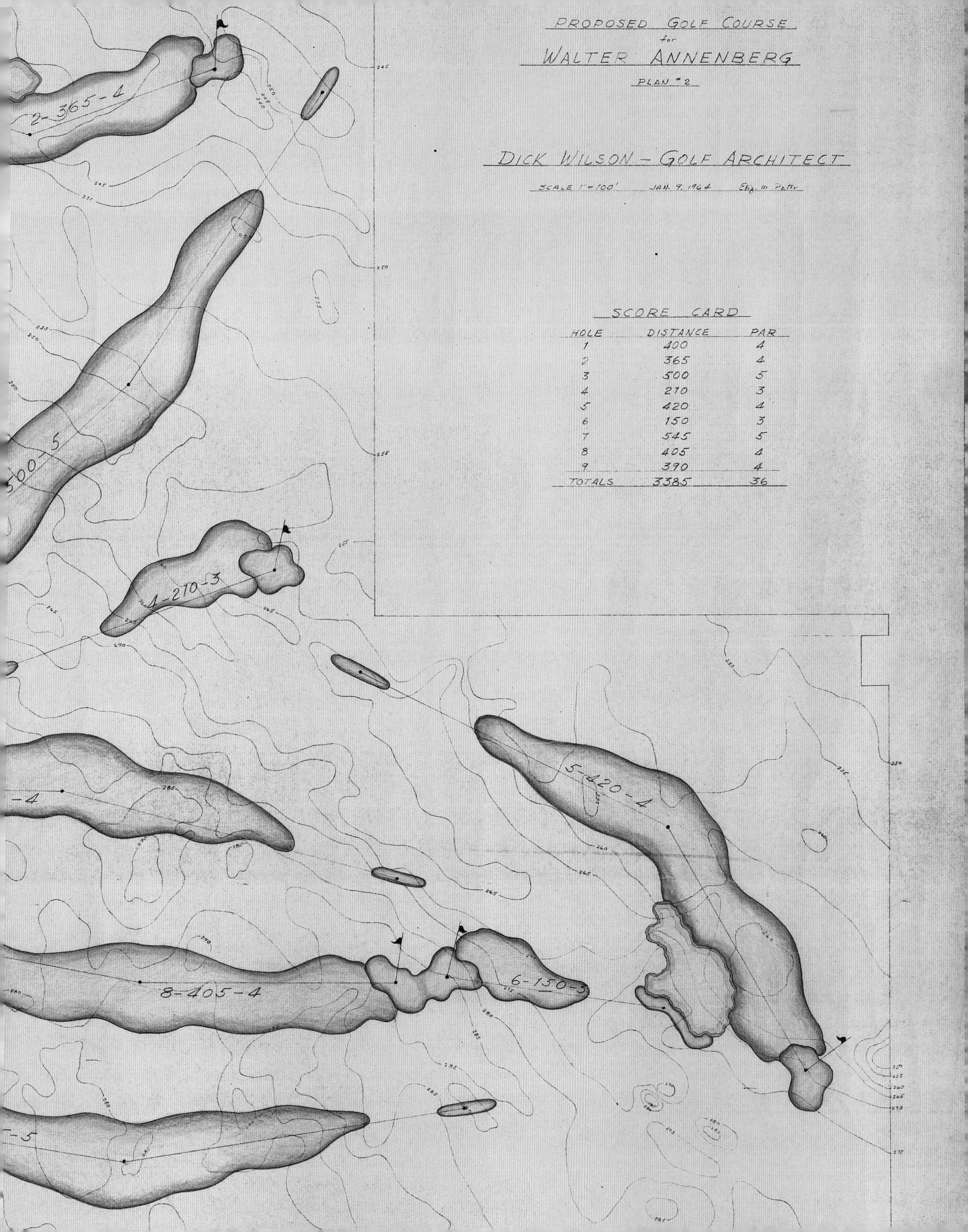

PROPOSED GOLF COURSE
for
WALTER ANNENBERG
PLAN #2
DICK WILSON - GOLF ARCHITECT
SCALE 1" = 100'
JAN. 9, 1964
SCORE CARD
HOLE DISTANCE PAR
1 400 4
2 365 4
3 500 5
4 210 3
5 420 4
6 150 3
7 545 5
8 405 4
9 390 4
TOTALS 3385 36
2-365-4
500-5
4-210-3
5-420-4
6-150-3
8-405-4

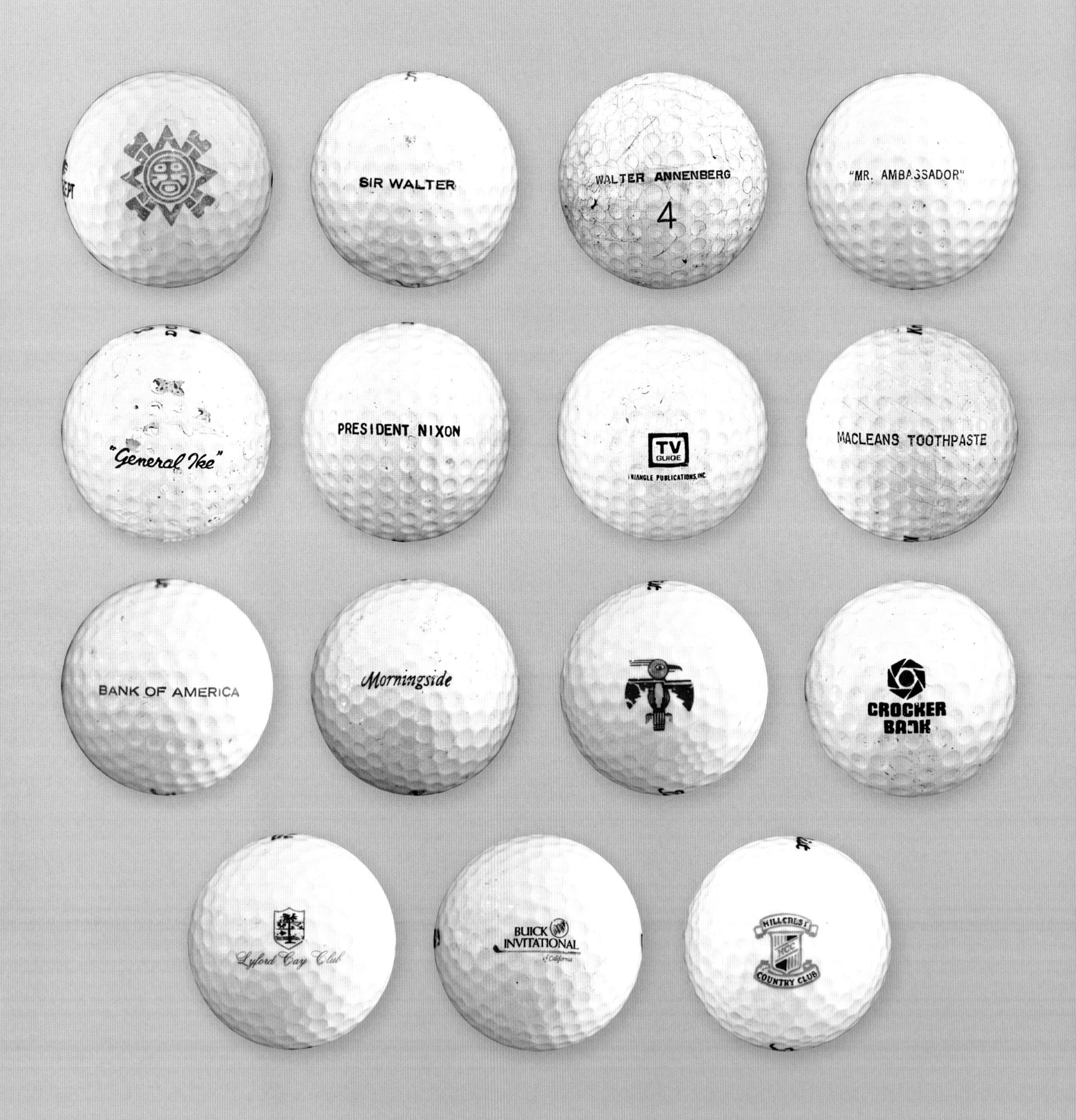
SIR WALTER
WALTER ANNENBERG
4
"MR. AMBASSADOR"
"General Ike"
PRESIDENT NIXON
TV GUIDE
MACLEANS TOOTHPASTE
BANK OF AMERICA
Morningside
CROCKER
Lyford Cay Club
BUICK INVITATIONAL
HILLCREST
HCC
COUNTRY CLUB

Many of the golfers who played at Sunnylands brought personalized golf balls. Some were shared with the Annenbergs, but hundreds of them ended up at the bottom of lakes. When the lakes were drained, historic balls were collected. These pages show a selection.

Lee beamed like a sunflower--all aglow in a bright yellow outfit, complementing her California golden complexion and blonde hair.

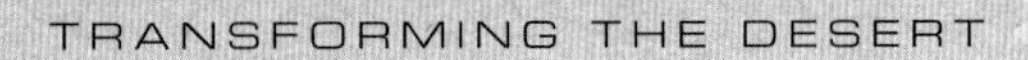

These pages from columnist Gloria Etting's scrapbook also record the plantings around the house in 1968. Etting's personal thoughts in these captions are invaluable archival material that brings Sunnylands to life.

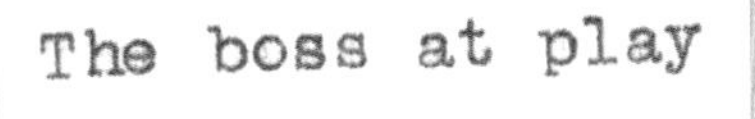

Below Walter and Leonore lunch with friends at the Chinese Pavilion in 1977.

Opposite Floral wallpaper decorates the walls of the women's locker room.

Opposite The sculpture *Birds of Welcome,* by Canadian artist Art Price, greets visitors as they approach the house on the main driveway.

Above Embroidered and appliquéd napkins with golf themes were used for outdoor lunches and afternoon drinks.

Left This view of the Chinese Pavilion in 2015 illustrates the current emphasis on sustainable practices for water use.

Overleaf The Chinese Pavilion is a folly, much like the mock Egyptian pyramids, Roman temples, and ruined abbeys on British country estates.

POWER AND POLITICS AT PLAY

Opposite Nancy and Ronald Reagan relax poolside on December 31, 1981. At this moment in the history of the estate, topiary trees can be seen near the house, and grass has replaced the original bougainvillea atop the bermed wall.

Overleaf Pages from the guest books provide a glimpse of the people who visited Sunnylands and their reactions to the experience. Nancy Reagan wrote, "I love being so spoiled!—but it makes going back to being a pumpkin hard."

For more than three decades, the Annenbergs brought people of power, influence, and celebrity together at Sunnylands for relaxation and celebration. Marcia French recalls a party attended by Dinah Shore, Frank and Barbara Sinatra, Gerald and Betty Ford, and Bob and Dolores Hope, all of whom had been immortalized with prominent Coachella Valley roads named in their honor. Shore looked around the room and commented, "The party can start—all the streets are here."

The welcoming of the political elite began immediately upon completion of the house. During the first week of the Annenbergs' residence at Sunnylands, former president Dwight and Mamie Eisenhower visited the newly finished estate. Eisenhower was an avid golfer and happily played golf on the course. He was surprised that there were no palm trees (the signature tree of the Palm Springs area) on the grounds. Responding to this comment, the Annenbergs had two *Washingtonia robusta* palms planted and called them the "Eisenhower Palms." Dwight Eisenhower also took advantage of the lakes stocked with bass, bluegill, and catfish for catch-and-release fly fishing. Shortly after his April 1966 visit, Eisenhower wrote: "Dear Mrs. Annenberg, Your dinner party Friday evening was one of the most enjoyable I have ever attended. Without exception I found every guest interesting and in spite of my passion for going to bed early I must confess that I was still sitting at the table at 11:15!"

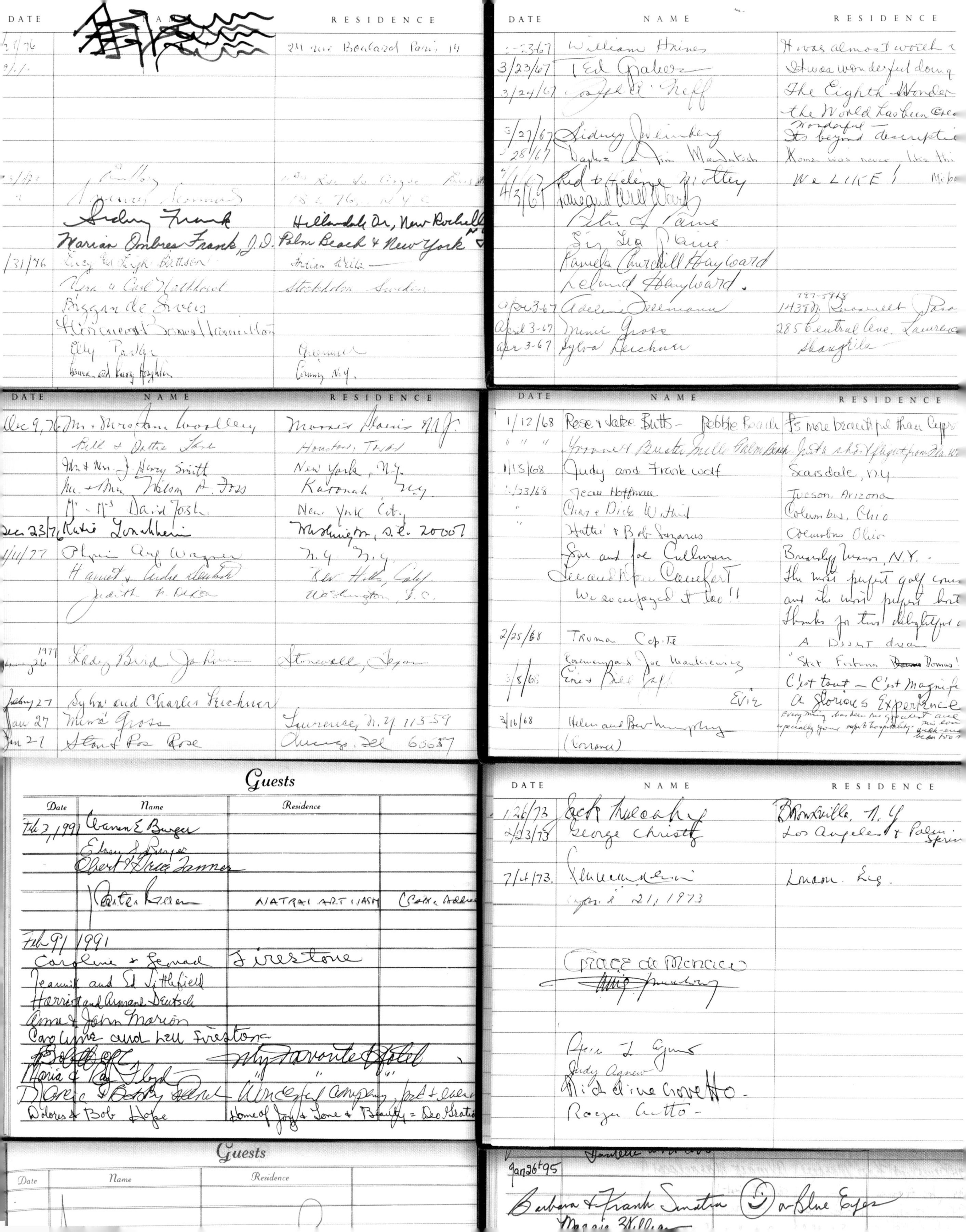

DATE	NAME	RESIDENCE
[illegible]	[illegible]	24 rue Boulard Paris 14
	Sidney Frank	Hillandale Dr., New Rochelle
	Marian Ombres Frank, J.D.	Palm Beach & New York
1/31/76	Lucy [illegible] Leigh Battson	
	Vera & Carl Nathhorst	Stockholm Sweden
	Elly Parker	Greenwich
		Corning N.Y.

DATE	NAME	RESIDENCE
3/23/67	William Haines	It was almost worth it
3/23/67	Ted Graber	It was wonderful doing
3/24/67	Joseph R. Neff	The Eighth Wonder the World has been Created
3/27/67	Sidney [illegible]	Wonderful — Its beyond description
3/28/67	Daphne & [illegible] MacIntosh	Home was never like this
4/1/67	Red & Helene Motley	We LIKE!
4/3/67	[illegible]	
	Peter S. Paine	
	[illegible] Paine	
	Pamela Churchill Hayward	
	Leland Hayward.	
Apr 3-67	Adeline [illegible]	1439 N. Roxanne [illegible] Pasa
April 3-67	Mimi Gross	285 Central Ave. Lawrence
Apr 3-67	Sylvia [illegible]	Shangrila

DATE	NAME	RESIDENCE
Dec 9, 76	Mr. & Mrs. Tom Woolley	Morris Plains N.J.
	Bill & Dottie [illegible]	Houston, Texas
	Mr. & Mrs. J. Henry Smith	New York, N.Y.
	Mr. & Mrs. Nelson A. Foss	Katonah N.Y.
	Mr. & Mrs. David Josh.	New York City.
Dec 23/76	Katie [illegible]	Washington, D.C. 20007
1/11/77	[illegible] Wagner	N.Y. N.Y.
	Harriet & [illegible]	Bev. Hills, Calif.
	Judith [illegible]	Washington, D.C.
1977 Jan 26	Lady Bird Johnson	Stonewall, Texas
Jan 27	Sylvia and Charles [illegible]	
Jan 27	Mimi Gross	Lawrence, N.Y. 11559
Jan 27	[illegible] Rose	Chicago, Ill 60657

DATE	NAME	RESIDENCE
1/12/68	Rose & Jake Butts - Pebble Beach	It's more beautiful than Capri
" " "	[illegible] Buster Mills Palm Beach	[illegible]
1/13/68	Judy and Frank Wolf	Scarsdale, N.Y.
1/23/68	Jean Hoffman	Tucson, Arizona
"	Char & Dick [illegible]	Columbus, Ohio
"	Hattie & Bob Lazarus	Columbus Ohio
	[illegible] and Joe Cullman	Briarcliff Manor, N.Y.
	[illegible] Comfort	The most perfect golf course and the most perfect host
	We so enjoyed it too!!	Thanks for this delightful [illegible]
2/25/68	Truman Capote	A Desert dream
	Rosemary & Joe Mankiewicz	"Stet Fortuna Domus"
3/8/68	Evie & Bill [illegible]	C'est tout — C'est Magnifique
	Evie	A Glorious Experience
3/16/68	Helen and Bev Murphy (Torrance)	Everything has been the greatest and especially your superb hospitality. [illegible]

Guests

Date	Name	Residence	
Feb 2, 1991	Warren E. Burger		
	Elvera S. Burger		
	Robert & Grace Tanner		
	[illegible]	NATIONAL ART [illegible]	[illegible]
Feb 9, 1991	Caroline & Leonard	Firestone	
	Jeannie and Ed Littlefield		
	Harriet and Armand Deutsch		
	Anne & John Marion		
	Caroline and [illegible] Firestone		
	[illegible]	My favorite Hotel	
	Maria & [illegible] Floyd	" " "	
	[illegible] & Bobby [illegible]	Wonderful company, food & [illegible]	
	Dolores & Bob Hope	Home of Joy & Love & Beauty = Deo Gratias	

DATE	NAME	RESIDENCE
1/26/73	Jack Mulcahy	Bronxville, N.Y.
2/23/73	George Christy	Los Angeles & Palm Springs
7/4/73	[illegible]	London. Eng.
	April 21, 1973	
	Grace de Monaco	
	[illegible]	
	[illegible]	
	Judy Agnew	
	Micheline [illegible]	
	Roger [illegible]	

Guests

Date	Name	Residence	

Jan 26th 95	Barbara & Frank Sinatra	Ol' Blue Eyes

DATE
NAME
RESIDENCE
Wallis Annenberg
Best Thanksgiving, ever!!!
Love and Thank You!
Dolores Hope
Such beauty – such love
Too beautiful To be True.
Harriet & Armand S. Deutsch
Great to be with you!
Again....
Ronald Reagan
L.A. Calif.
Nancy Reagan
William French Smith
Dear sister – you live in Paradise!
Dallas Tex
SACEUR – NATO
Pat Haig
What a marvelous day!
Elizabeth R
February 27th 1983
Philip
Betty and Bill Wilson
Los Angeles
L.A.
Beverly Hills, Calif
A sad occasion gave us the happiness to know and enjoy the friendship of a generous man and his charming family
Imperial Court
Tehran – IRAN
Guests
Date
Name
Residence
Thank you for your hospitality and friendship!
Hillary Rodham Clinton
1.26.95
Betty and Jerry Ford
1/26/95
Elizabeth Dole
Washington, DC
Philadelphia, PA
Glorious as Ever!
1/18/03
Rosalynn Carter
Plains, Ga.
January 19th, 2003

President-elect Richard Nixon and his wife Pat stayed at Sunnylands following his November 1968 election. The next month the Republican Governors Association gathered to celebrate Nixon's victory and the Annenbergs hosted a dinner at Sunnylands. There were "thirty-three governors and their spouses, the president-elect and daughter, Tricia, who filled in for the ailing Pat Nixon, and vice president–elect Agnew, whom Walter then did not know." It was during that December visit that Nixon asked Walter to serve as the Ambassador to the Court of St. James's. In January 1974, Nixon drafted his State of the Union address while staying in the guest room that later became the library called the Room of Memories. But just nine months later, he returned to Sunnylands following the Watergate scandal and his resignation as president. He wrote in the guest book: "When you're down, you find out who your *real* friends are."

President Gerald Ford continued the tradition of presidents spending time at Sunnylands. He and Betty first signed the guest book in 1974, when he wrote: "A wonderful visit in every way. We loved it." The Fords were frequent guests once they purchased a home in Rancho Mirage. Sixty-one visits were recorded, and the Annenbergs contributed financial support for the founding of the Betty Ford Center to provide treatment for people with alcohol and drug addictions.

Ronald and Nancy Reagan began visiting Sunnylands in 1967. While he served as California governor, they often came to stay. In 1967 Nancy wrote: "You make it hard to go back to the mansion," referring to the governor's mansion in Sacramento.

Following Reagan's election as president in November 1980, he and Nancy celebrated with the Annenbergs at their New Year's Eve party and then enjoyed New Year's Day 1981 together. The Reagans subsequently spent every New Year's during his presidency at Sunnylands. The New Year's Eve party, which began with twenty people and a movie in 1966, grew into a formal affair for ninety to one hundred who toasted the occasion with Schramsberg sparkling wine and danced to the music of the Tony Rose Orchestra.

Reagan played golf once a year at Sunnylands. As his wife noted, you need to play golf more than once a year to be good at the game. Reagan was a duffer, and his frustration with his game can be seen in many photographs taken on the Sunnylands course.

In addition to using Sunnylands as an escape from Washington's worries, Reagan on occasion brought members of his cabinet to the desert to meet with him away from the public eye. In the privacy of Sunnylands' two hundred acres, President Reagan could speak without distraction to people such as Secretary of State George Shultz, who credits one of those golf course conversations with leading to the Tax Reform Act of 1986. The Canada–United States Free Trade Agreement, a precursor to the North American Free Trade Agreement, (NAFTA), was signed at Sunnylands on January 2, 1988. While seated in the Room of Memories, Reagan watched Soviet Premier Mikhail Gorbachev on television speaking to the American people about nuclear disarmament. Reagan's speech on the same topic was broadcast in the Soviet Union on the same day.

George H. W. Bush brought his presidency to Sunnylands as well. In March 1990, the President and First Lady were scheduled to spend a restful weekend with the Annenbergs, but just a few days before the visit, there was talk of the Japanese government closing its markets to the United States. Bush contacted Walter for a favor, asking him to host a formal dinner for Toshiki Kaifu of Japan during his visit, while the White House scheduled a special meeting with the Japanese Prime Minister. The ceremonial dinner took place at Sunnylands hosted by the President and First Lady and presented by Walter and Leonore. Leonore's days as chief of protocol for Ronald Reagan served her well, as she'd been given only three days to plan an official dinner. During that same weekend stay, President Bush announced the Annenbergs' gift of $50 million to the United Negro College Fund, then the largest gift in the history of the UNCF. From 1994 until 2007, there would be an additional fifteen visits by the Bushes to Sunnylands.

On February 14, 1995, President William J. Clinton visited Sunnylands, three weeks after First Lady Hillary Clinton had come. Photographs show Leonore and Walter (both dressed in Valentine red) discussing their painting collection with Bill Clinton. George W. Bush visited Sunnylands

Opposite Bob Hope does a little soft-shoe on December 31, 1982.

for a fundraiser prior to his election as president in 2000. First Lady Laura Bush came in 2004 for a lunch held in her honor by Leonore Annenberg.

President Barack Obama, the eighth president to visit Sunnylands, used the estate to meet with President Xi Jinping of China in June 2013—the meeting that laid the groundwork for their personal relationship, which resulted in key agreements on climate change. King Abdullah II of Jordan met with President Obama in February 2014. In February 2016, President Obama hosted a two-day summit for ten leaders of ASEAN (Association of Southeast Asian Nations) to strengthen the United States–ASEAN strategic partnership on political, security, and economic issues. President Obama has escaped Washington, D.C., to play golf at Sunnylands on three additional occasions.

Many other American political leaders have visited Sunnylands over the years. Secretary of State Henry Kissinger made four visits in the 1980s and 1990s, while Secretary of State George Shultz came sixteen times between 1985 and 2007. Walter and Leonore were particularly fond of Colin and Alma Powell and loved it when Colin arrived and announced: "Mom and Pop—we're home!"

In 1979, the Annenbergs offered refuge to the mother and sister of the exiled shah of Iran, who fled their house in Beverly Hills when demonstrators encamped there. The hospitality extended to the exiles' fourteen dogs, pet birds, and a personal veterinarian. They stayed two weeks at one of the cottages and signed the guest book: "A sad occasion gave us the happiness to know and enjoy the friendship of a generous man and his charming family. Thank you, Mr. Ambassador."

Business leaders and philanthropists such as David Rockefeller, Warren Buffett, Edmond and Lily Safra, and Bill and Melinda Gates came in the 1990s. Literary and media figures were always part of the crowd. Truman Capote came in 1968 followed by Newton Minow, Ann Landers, and Sidney Sheldon. Television anchors, including Barbara Walters, Peter Jennings, Andrea Mitchell, and Diane Sawyer, were guests in later years.

Entertainment icons came to sing and play. Neighbor Frank Sinatra was married to Barbara Marx at Sunnylands in July 1976. Bob and Dolores Hope came a total of fifty times between 1975 and 2005. Actors Kirk Douglas and Gregory Peck, singers Beverly Sills and Michael Feinstein, comedian George Burns, conductor Zubin Mehta, designer Oscar de la Renta, and artist Helen Frankenthaler have all visited the estate.

Not to be left out were the leaders in the museum world. Thomas Hoving, Philippe de Montebello, and William Luers from the Metropolitan Museum of Art in New York were frequent guests. Anne d'Harnoncourt of the Philadelphia Museum of Art visited six times after the Annenberg announcement of the gift of their Impressionist and Post-Impressionist paintings to the Met. Andrea Rich of the Los Angeles County Museum of Art, J. Carter Brown of the National Gallery of Art, James Wood of the Art Institute of Chicago, and John Walsh of the Getty all spent time at Sunnylands.

In the social arena, Brooke Astor, Betsy Bloomingdale, Norman and Dorothy Chandler, Charles and Jayne Wrightsman, and John and Anne Marion engaged with other prominent guests. Astor proclaimed that an invitation to the Sunnylands annual New Year's Eve party "was the greatest invitation one could ever have." Anne Rowe, Director of Sunnylands Collections and Exhibitions, notes in *The Pleasure of Your Company*: "Former guests reported that each and every detail of hospitality was extraordinarily custom-tailored to individual visitors."

The Annenbergs developed a deep personal relationship with the British royal family during their tenure in London. As a result, many members of the royal family were guests at Sunnylands. In March 1974, while Prince Charles was in San Diego during his service in the British Navy, the Annenbergs invited him to Sunnylands. He stayed for the weekend and wrote in the guest book: "You left all this to go to England?" The Annenbergs attended the wedding of Prince Charles and Lady Diana Spencer in July 1981.

Queen Elizabeth II and Prince Philip visited Sunnylands on February 27, 1983, while on a ten-day goodwill tour of California. They had lunch in the Annenberg dining room, where the Queen noted the collection of Flora Danica china displayed there. She indicated that she also had a collection of Flora Danica but said, ". . . Walter has more than I do." The weather was rainy and cold, not at all typical of the desert in season. The Queen lamented that she brought the weather from England as Walter took her on a tour of the grounds in an open golf cart.

The luncheon for the Queen was intimate but formal. Eighteen guests sat at two tables with the Queen seated between Walter and Gerald Ford, and Prince Philip between Leonore and Betty Ford. The rack of lamb entrée was paired with a 1966 Chateau Lafite Rothschild, while the maple soufflé dessert was complemented by a 1970 Dom

Mamie and Dwight Eisenhower were among the first visitors to Sunnylands. They were also part of the weekend festivities documented by Gloria Etting in 1968.

Perignon. Eight Boehm porcelain roses, named for Leonore Annenberg, decorated the Queen's table.

Prime Minister Margaret Thatcher first visited Sunnylands in 1991 and then returned for an additional four visits through 1998. She recalled Walter's diplomatic impact on the United Kingdom: "He did so much to strengthen the relationship and the natural ties which already existed . . . Walter could, as the saying goes, 'walk with kings and not lose the common touch' . . . He has that marvelous generosity of spirit that is America." Thatcher's visit in 1995 prompted the Annenbergs to build the wall that lines two sides of the estate, after a blight killed the pink blossoming oleander bushes that were there. To ensure privacy and a sense of seclusion for future guests, the Annenbergs had a concrete block wall installed and painted pink to match the roof of the house. The pink wall immediately became a desert icon, making local residents that much more interested in what went on behind it. Other British prime ministers also visited Sunnylands: James Callaghan in 1989, and John Major three times between 1998 and 2001.

But the Annenbergs' home was also a place for family. "The ambassador was fond of saying that house guests should come every other weekend so that he had time to enjoy his property also," said estate manager Linda Brooks. So the grandchildren grew up visiting Sunnylands for Christmas, Easter, and many other occasions in between. Photographs show Walter reading *'Twas the Night Before Christmas* to his grandchildren and Easter egg hunts for the little ones. Leonore's daughter Diane Deshong says, "Although much of consequence occurred at Sunnylands, it is important to remember that it was a family home . . . Mom loved having all the children, grandchildren, and great-grandchildren visit." Some of the grandchildren share memories of riding bikes and driving golf carts, sometimes not carefully, landing in a lake or bunker.

Whether a president, a celebrity, or a grandchild, visitors to Sunnylands experienced an unparalleled ambience that felt otherworldly. Ambassador Charles Price said in his 1978 toast: "I hope for permission to eventually enter the Pearly Gates. And I also give thanks for having been to Sunnylands first."

Opposite clockwise Gerald and Betty Ford, George W. Bush, and Leonore at a Sunnylands reception in May 2000. Hillary Clinton visiting with Walter in January 1995. Richard and Pat Nixon with their granddaughter Jennie Eisenhower and Leonore in April 1979. Bill Clinton with the Annenbergs on Valentine's Day 1995. Charles Price, Gerald Ford, Bob Hope, Prince Andrew, and Walter in 1994. Gerald Ford and Walter with two other golfers at the Chinese Pavilion in March 1978.

Above Dwight Eisenhower with the Annenbergs in front of the Beaucarnea tree in 1968.

Overleaf Nancy and Ronald Reagan dance to a mariachi band on January 1, 1983.

NEW YEAR'S EVE AT SUNNYLANDS

An interview with Carol Price, April 2016

Carol Swanson Price grew up within the Annenberg circle because her mother and father were close friends of Walter Annenberg. As a young woman, and later as the wife of Charles Price, who served as Ambassador to the Court of St. James's from 1983 to 1989, Carol frequently visited Sunnylands. "After we bought our first desert house, I realized this was a major mistake because we could no longer stay at Sunnylands!" she said in this recent interview. "I always thought of the Annenbergs as 'life enhancers'—those are two words that aren't often put together." Here she recalls the legendary New Year's Eve parties for which Sunnylands was well known.

"New Year's Eve was spectacular. Cocktails started at 8:15 p.m., with dinner at 9:00 p.m. House Manager Michael Comerford was always at the front door. And then Lee would swoop in and greet everyone graciously. We would move through the atrium, pick up our seating information, and wander over to the living room for the reception.

Michel Venuat, the French chef, made the most wonderful hors d'oeuvres—always beautiful, and smaller than a quarter. Peanut butter and bacon on croissant, cheese onion puffs, as well as ham and pickle rolled in Boursin were favorites. Glasses of white wine and Schramsberg sparkling wine were always passed, but there were many vodka drinkers, too. The women really went out of their way to look glamorous. Designers like Oscar de la Renta, Bill Blass, Givenchy, and Balmain were represented. Mrs. Annenberg had thought about her dress long in advance. It was the kind of party that you'd buy a dress for. And if you had jewelry, this was one place you could wear it. Designs by David Webb, Harry Winston, and Van Cleef & Arpels were sparkling throughout the room.

Lee separated couples at the dinner tables to encourage lively conversation. She had an unerring eye for detail. She always selected different tablecloths, and the flowers were gorgeous. There were party favors placed on the woman's plate before dessert. Cobalt blue and gold Halcyon clocks, silver armada dishes, paperweights, and the Halcyon box

with Sunnylands emblem were all shared with guests. Everything was so perfect, but not perfect in a stiff way.

The Annenbergs always had wonderful music. For many years it was Tony Rose and his orchestra. Quite often Dolores Hope sang, and also Gayle Wilson, wife of Governor Pete Wilson, who has a really pretty voice. My husband, Charlie, would sing with Merv Griffin, and that would be hilarious.

Walter and Lee loved to dance. They looked so in love. George Shultz would dance with all the ladies. It was fun for all the couples to mix up their dance partners.

There was just a buzz. You know when something clicks . . . there was that sound of a party clicking."

Opposite The Reagans attended the Annenbergs' New Year's Eve parties every year that Ronald Reagan was president.

Overleaf The Annenbergs and the Reagans, in decidedly eighties fashions, took to the dance floor on New Year's Eve 1985.

December 31, 1982

Lee and Walter
Another happy new year, thanks to you - Fondly - Nancy & Ron

December 31, 1987

New Year's Eve 1987

December 31, 1983

Dear Lee and Walter -
Another happy new year, thanks to you - our love
Nancy & Ron

December 31, 1984

Dear Lee & Walter - Of course it was a happy new year -
We were together. Love
Nancy & Ron

December 31, 1986

MANAGING SUNNYLANDS

An interview with Michael Comerford, March 2016

Michael Comerford served as House Manager for thirty-five years, from 1974 to 2009. During that time he oversaw a staff of fourteen: four butlers, three maids, three kitchen staff, two laundresses, and two guest attendants. Additional staff were hired for special events.

How did the Annenbergs plan for weekend guests?

Weekend events were planned by Mrs. Annenberg, who worked with me and the estate manager to ensure that the two secretaries knew what documents to prepare, maintenance employees knew how many tables to set up, and the horticulturist knew to replace the flowers. She then worked directly with me and chef Michel Venuat when planning the menu. Finally, Mrs. Annenberg and I would choose the linens, flatware, and table ornaments.

What kind of information was provided to guests for a weekend visit to Sunnylands?

Guests were thoughtfully chosen to form a cohesive weekend group. Mrs. Annenberg often said that one of the keys to good entertaining was choosing a group of interesting people. Invitations were sent out well in advance, and the schedule, with proposed activities and suggested dress, was forwarded to guests ahead of time.

On arrival, guests found in their rooms a summary of the accomplishments and interests of the other guests. Breakfast cards were placed in each room, the butler collected them at night, and then breakfast was served on color-coordinated trays in the guest rooms. The ladies had breakfast in bed, while gentlemen received breakfast at the desk.

The final weekend schedule of events was placed in each guest room and included the names of all guests and their guest room phone numbers; a list of the group activities, locations, and times (lunch, golf, cocktails, dinner, movie); and a list of activities to enjoy during free time (tennis, fishing, golfing, sunning, swimming, backgammon, football).

Newsweek and *Time* magazines on topics of interest and the guest's newspaper of choice were placed in the rooms. If an interesting article came up in a conversation, Mrs. Annenberg would mention that her secretary had a copy of it, and if the guest requested, the article was copied and delivered to their room in a sealed envelope.

Mrs. Annenberg arranged the seating plan, a task she executed thoughtfully. She also checked the tables after the place cards were laid down to make certain that the seating was correct.

How did Walter and Leonore spend their time during an average weekend with visitors at Sunnylands?

On Friday afternoon, they would greet guests on arrival and converse with them. Dinner was casual that evening. On Saturday they would join the guests for golf, lunch, and, when royalty visited, afternoon tea. That night there would be a formal dinner. After dinner, guests would have a tour of the Room of Memories or the paintings collection and enjoy a movie in the Game Room. On Sunday, there would be lunch with the guests before they departed. Their cars were washed and filled with gas.

How did guests dress for a typical weekend visit?

Friday night, the arrival night, was usually casual, but the Annenbergs required a jacket at all times in the dining room. A typical outfit for gentlemen would be a collared, button-down shirt, a blazer, and slacks. Gentlemen wore a dark suit and tie for Saturday night while ladies wore cocktail dresses or dressy pantsuits. Lunch attire was casual: Gentlemen typically wore pants and golf shirts. Ladies could wear dress shorts and a blouse. If guests were scheduled to golf after lunch, they could use the locker rooms to change into golf attire.

What china, linen, and flatware was used for the weekend?

When the Annenbergs were alone, they used either the Rothschild Bird china by Herend or the Cheviot Green china by Minton. During the weekends, the Minton was used with Georg Jensen flatware for the arrival dinner. During the formal Saturday dinner, Flora Danica china was used with silver-gilt flatware.

What schedule did you follow as house manager?

My day started at 7:00 a.m. I turned off the alarms and did a walkthrough of the house to make sure everything was in order. Breakfast was served to staff at 7:30 a.m. and to the Annenbergs when they called for it, usually around 8:30 a.m. After meeting with any staff who needed specific instructions for the day, I took lunch and dinner requests from the Ambassador and Mrs. Annenberg. At 11:30 a.m., staff ate lunch, and at 12:30 p.m. the Annenbergs were served lunch. The afternoon was set aside for running errands. By 6:30 or 7:00 p.m., I would be either in the ambassador's office or the dining room to oversee the dinner service.

Each week, I had a meeting with the maintenance engineer with a list of service requests to be completed, but if anything was needed in an emergency, I had it taken care of immediately. When there was a major weekend planned, I met with all the staff on Wednesday. I spoke with the maids about linens, the horticulturist about flower arrangements in the house and the guest quarters, and the chef and kitchen staff to keep them updated. I worked with the floor butlers and the laundress, who would need to recruit extra help during a busy weekend.

Every second Wednesday was silver-cleaning day. All of the silver in the main house was brought to the pantry for cleaning.

My day ended when the Annenbergs retired for the evening. At that time, I put out the lights, bid the Annenbergs good night, and turned on the alarm system.

Michael Comerford, third from right, stands with staff as they prepare to start serving on New Year's Eve 1982.

Right President Richard Nixon gave this sixteen-piece set of personalized golf clubs with a handwritten note to Walter. Special visitors to Sunnylands who needed clubs to play the course were surprised by the loan of this set.

Opposite George H.W. Bush loved to fish in the lakes. In this 1995 photograph, he showed off his catch before releasing it back into the water.

Overleaf Barbara Bush and Leonore offer encouragement while on the golf course in 1990.

Pages 214–15 Walter's golfing buddies, including George H. W. Bush, celebrate a successful putt.

WESTERN

Above Prince Charles joins the Annenbergs for an announcement about Operation Raleigh in 1984.

Opposite Queen Elizabeth II and Prince Philip arrive for lunch on February 27, 1983, during a goodwill tour of California.

OFFICIAL LUNCHEON LIST
February 27, 1983

Mr. & Mrs. Walter Annenberg
Rancho Mirage, California

HONORING
HER MAJESTY QUEEN ELIZABETH II
and
HIS ROYAL HIGHNESS THE PRINCE PHILIP
DUKE OF EDINBURGH

BRITISH

HER MAJESTY QUEEN ELIZABETH II

HIS ROYAL HIGHNESS THE PRINCE PHILIP
Duke of Edinburgh

HIS EXCELLENCY SIR OLIVER WRIGHT AND LADY WRIGHT
British Ambassador to the United States

THE DUCHESS OF GRAFTON, G.C.V.O.
Mistress of the Robes

LADY SUSAN HUSSEY, C.V.O.
Lady-in-Waiting

THE RIGHT HONORABLE SIR PHILIP MOORE,
K.D.B.,K.C.V.O.,D.M.G.

MR. AND MRS. GEORGE F. FINLAYSON
Consul General, Los Angeles

MR. ROBERT FELLOWES
Assistant Private Secretary

MR. MICHAEL SHEA
Press Secretary to The Queen

AMERICAN

THE HONORABLE AND MRS. WALTER H. ANNENBERG
Former Ambassador to the Court of St. James's

PRESIDENT GERALD FORD AND MRS. FORD
Former President of the United States of America

THE HONORABLE MICHAEL DEAVER AND MRS. DEAVER
Deputy Chief of Staff and Assistant to the President

THE HONORABLE JOHN J. LOUIS, JR. AND MRS. LOUIS
U.S. Ambassador to the United Kingdom of Great Britain

THE HONORABLE SELWA ROOSEVELT
Chief of Protocol

LUNCHEON SEATING PLAN
February 27, 1983

SUNNYLANDS

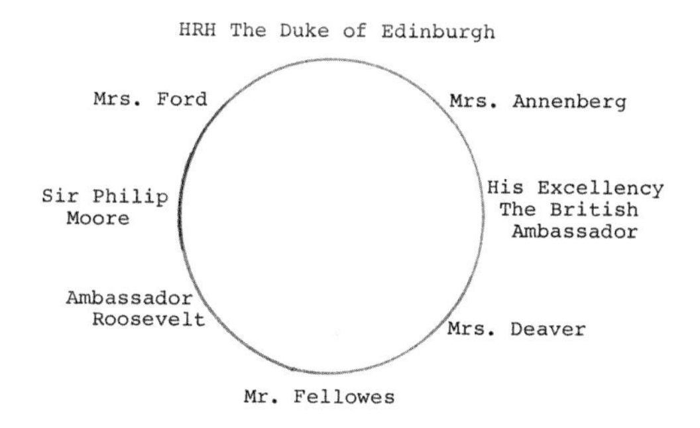

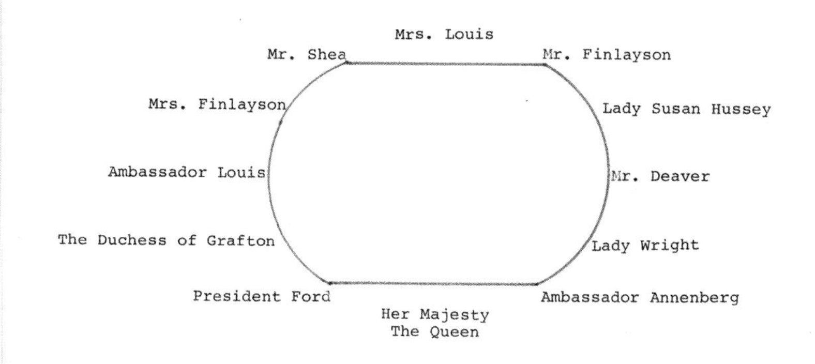

Mousselines of Salmon
Cucumbers Sauce Verte

Rack of Lamb

String Beans Glazed Carrots
Pommes Parisienne

Soufflé à l'Erable

Bernkasteler Doctor Riesling
1979 Auslese
Chateau Lafite Rothschild 1966
Dom Perignon Magnums 1970

February 27, 1983

This collage of items from the Queen's luncheon includes the seating plan, menu, text for Walter's toast, and a photograph of the table setting.

Opposite The guest list reflects strict adherence to protocol. As Walter said, "If we asked four old friends, we'd make enemies of forty. We thought it prudent to just have the official party."

YOUR MAJESTY AND YOUR ROYAL HIGHNESS:

YOUR VISIT HERE AT SUNNYLANDS IS INDEED HISTORIC.

YOUR PRESENCE BRIGHTLY REKINDLES OUR 5 1/2 YEARS IN BRITAIN - CERTAINLY THE PROUDEST YEARS FOR LEE AND ME.

WE CONTINUE TO REMEMBER THE GRACIOUS MANNER IN WHICH WE WERE RECEIVED BY THE ROYAL FAMILY AND THE PEOPLE OF BRITAIN; AND WE CONTINUE TO BE GRATEFUL FOR THE RELATIONSHIP EXISTING BETWEEN GREAT BRITAIN AND THE UNITED STATES.

WILL YOU RISE AND JOIN ME IN A TOAST TO HER MAJESTY THE QUEEN AND HIS ROYAL HIGHNESS PRINCE PHILIP - THE TOAST:

THE QUEEN AND PRINCE PHILIP

GETTING MARRIED AT SUNNYLANDS

"Being married at Sunnylands was marvelous—an unbelievable experience! It was a very hot July day in the desert and the wedding was a surprise to our guests. They thought they were coming for an engagement party. Lee Annenberg and Harriet Deutsch planned the flowers, so the house was filled with white gardenias, white roses, white chrysanthemums, and white orchids. It was simply spectacular to see. I was so fortunate to be married to Frank for twenty-two years—he was always generous, warm, kind, sweet, and so adorable to me, and he made me feel totally fulfilled. I have been a very lucky lady and have no regrets. If I had to do it all over again, I would do it exactly the same again."

—Barbara Sinatra, 2016

Below The Sinatras and the Annenbergs in a formal wedding portrait on July 11, 1976.

Above left Kirk and Anne Douglas with Barbara Sinatra at the Sinatra compound following the Sunnylands wedding. Frank gave Barbara a deep-blue Rolls Royce "to match her eyes" as a wedding gift.

Above right Kirk Douglas and Gregory Peck arrive.

Below Frank, in a white suit, and Barbara, in a beige chiffon Halston, cut the cake.

Top left Grace, Princess of Monaco, and Walter, in conversation on the terrace in 1973.

Top right Barbara Walters was a frequent guest in the 1990s.

Above left Brooke Astor joined the Annenbergs for dinner on New Year's Eve 1988.

Above right Colin and Alma Powell loved visiting Sunnylands.

Opposite Truman Capote and two of Walter's sisters, Lita Hazen (left) and Evelyn Jaffe Hall, strike a pose for the camera during a visit in 1968.

Sunday, March 24th spread before us with more rays of sunshine following a cool night. The temperature rose to over eighty degrees by midday. Amplified dance music boomed from an FM station and we all broke into silly and exaggerated frug routines on the terrace.

Above A little midday dancing, recalled in a scrapbook.

Opposite Walter and Leonore rest near the pool following a weekend of guests.

Overleaf Leonore joined her guests in the swimming pool during this 1968 weekend.

Walter's sister, Leta, came for lunch, attractive, slim and blonde, in a yellow slacks outfit. She smiles with the same warmth and love of people as Walter and the other sisters I have met. After another delicious lunch the afternoon fled, perhaps because we did exactly what we wanted--sunbathing, swimming, talking or staring at "Sunnylands" which occupies one's whole sense of being alive.

The Annenbergs bid farewell to President Ronald and First Lady Nancy Reagan as Marine One lifts off from the grounds of Sunnylands on January 2, 1984.

SUNNYLANDS TODAY

Opposite The connection between nature and art is established at Sunnylands Center & Gardens with the placement of Alberto Giacometti's *Bust of Diego on Stele III* against a view of Mt. San Jacinto.

It quickly became evident that the architecture of A. Quincy Jones, the interiors of William Haines, and the vision of their clients added up to something far more than a mere house. Sunnylands is an atmosphere, an ambience, a spirit—an oasis that invites contemplation and reflection, for which the Annenbergs had one more plan.

In 2001, Walter and Leonore finalized the document that established the Annenberg Foundation Trust at Sunnylands, with the intent to turn Sunnylands into the "Camp David of the West" and to make it available to the public. The directive was to create the Annenberg Retreat at Sunnylands, bringing together world leaders to promote world peace and facilitate international agreement. The estate was to be made available to the President of the United States, the Secretary of State, the bipartisan leadership of Congress, the Supreme Court, and other leaders for intimate, high-level retreats where experts from a host of sectors, with diverse perspectives, would engage in creative, ambitious problem-solving fostered by the unique atmosphere of the estate.

Following Walter's death in 2002 and Leonore's passing in 2009, the Trust began the process of making the Annenberg Retreat at Sunnylands a reality. Walter and Leonore's daughters and grandchildren govern the nonprofit organization. In 2010, they selected Geoffrey Cowan, former dean of the Annenberg School for Communication & Journalism at the University of Southern California, as the Trust's first president.

The launch of Sunnylands as a retreat center and public historic site in 2012 was accomplished under Cowan's leadership. Experts in a range of areas are now partnering with Sunnylands to find solutions to some of the most critical challenges that face the nation and the world in such fields as education, institutions of democracy, health, arts and culture, and the range of issues facing the Greater Pacific region, with a particular focus on China and Mexico. Those retreats and meetings have produced impressive results through partnerships with world-renowned institutions capable of achieving transformative outcomes. Sunnylands' location in California, recognized globally as a haven for creativity, diversity, and innovation, is also critical to its role.

Perhaps the most enduring contemporary image of Sunnylands is that of President Barack Obama walking alongside President Xi Jinping of China, both in their shirtsleeves, strolling across the green grounds on a brilliant summer day. This meeting between the presidents in June 2013 was exactly what the Annenbergs had envisioned, and cemented the reputation of Sunnylands as an important site on the world stage. The two men spent time together in this "shirtsleeves summit" and announced agreements on greenhouse gases and climate change following the meeting. The calm, pastoral beauty of Sunnylands provided the ideal environment for candid conversation between these leaders whose nations are occasionally at odds. In February 2016, President Obama again used Sunnylands to host a summit with the ten leaders of the Southeast Asian nations (ASEAN).

At the same time, more than ninety thousand people visit Sunnylands each year. Sunnylands has become a popular destination for those interested in art, architecture, interior and landscape design, and the history of the Annenbergs in the twentieth century. Sunnylands Center & Gardens, designed by Frederick Fisher & Partners and opened in 2012, is a contemporary answer to the midcentury house by A. Quincy Jones. The glass pavilion sits in a nine-acre garden inspired by the Impressionist paintings collected by the Annenbergs. Michael S. Smith designed the interior furnishings to create a welcoming public living room. Landscape architect James Burnett used arid-landscape plants to establish a twenty-first-century oasis that provokes a comparison with the water-intensive twentieth-century historic estate.

Sunnylands Center & Gardens has become a public gathering place where people of all ages can participate in a wide range of educational programs. As the starting point for tours of the house and grounds, the Center offers access to a piece of American history for a broad public. Formal learning opportunities are offered in classes, lectures, and workshops. Self-directed activities include a multi-media gallery, exhibitions, and the film *A Place Called Sunnylands*. Whether relaxing in the public space, practicing yoga on the Great Lawn, or taking a garden or bird walk, visitors benefit from the Annenbergs' generosity and can share in their hopeful vision for a peaceful world.

Above The Retreat Pavilion, designed by architect Frederick Fisher & Partners, provides meeting space for sixteen retreat participants on the historic estate.

Overleaf President Barack Obama and President Xi Jinping of China take time for a private discussion on the bench that was his gift to the Chinese president.

Pages 236–37 Chief of Protocol Peter Selfridge accompanies one of the participants into the historic house during the summit for leaders of Southeast Asian nations (ASEAN) in February 2016.

inping President of the
ma President of the
lands Annenberg Estate
June 7-8, 2013
亚的红杉

ANTON BAUER
190

100
HYTRON

HE PRESIDENT
ANOTE TONG
HSH
PRINCE ALBERT
OF MONACO

ELIZABETH
ECONOMY
ORVILLE
SCHELL

Opposite clockwise President Anote Tong of Kiribati and Prince Albert II of Monaco during the Rising Oceans retreat in October 2014. King Abdullah II of Jordan with President Obama in February 2014. The China Task Force retreat, held in January 2016, included Elizabeth Economy from the Council on Foreign Relations, Orville Schell who is director of U.S.–China Relations at the Asia Society, Michael Swaine of the Carnegie Endowment for International Peace, and Taylor Favrel. Former Secretary of State Condoleezza Rice and Jane Harman, president of the Woodrow Wilson International Center for Scholars, at the United States–Mexico retreat in March 2012. Bill Gates speaks with Trust President Geoffrey Cowan at the Math Education retreat in April 2012.

Above Jon Huntsman, chairman of the Atlantic Council and former U.S. Ambassador to China, took advantage of a quiet moment during the United States–China Track II retreat in January 2014.

Overleaf The Sunnylands Center & Gardens serves as the public welcome for tours of the estate and educational programs that expand an understanding of the Annenberg legacy.

Previous pages The public living room at the Center & Gardens was designed by Michael S. Smith. Its furnishings relate to but do not attempt to copy Haines's style in the historic house.

Above Supreme Court justice Anthony Kennedy takes a walk on the estate during the opening weekend in March 2012.

Opposite The reflecting pool designed by the Office of James Burnett adds the sound of water to the desert plantings.

Overleaf This view of the gardens during spring recalls the Annenbergs' collection of Impressionist paintings.

Pages 248–49 President Obama and President Xi stroll on the grounds of Sunnylands during their meeting in June 2013.

ACKNOWLEDGMENTS

As with most projects, numerous individuals contributed in diverse and immeasurable ways to the process of making this book a reality.

The board of trustees of the Annenberg Foundation Trust at Sunnylands supported the concept of the publication. Trustees are Wallis Annenberg, Lauren Bon, Diane Deshong, Howard Deshong III, Leonore Deshong, Elizabeth Kabler, Elizabeth Sorensen, Charles Annenberg Weingarten, and Gregory Annenberg Weingarten. Geoffrey Cowan, president of the Annenberg Foundation Trust at Sunnylands from 2009 to 2016, also provided encouragement and advice.

I took advantage of the expertise of Sunnylands staff including the archival knowledge of Anne Rowe, director of collections and exhibitions; Kacey Donner, curatorial assistant; Frank Lopez, librarian and archivist; Daniel Modlin, photo archivist; and Mary Velez, art handler. I also benefited from the editing and communications skills of Geoffrey Baum, director of communications and public affairs; Ken Chavez, deputy director of communications and public affairs; Susan Davis, editorial director; and Ashley Santana, editorial assistant.

In addition, several individuals and organizations provided important assistance, including Karen Baumgartner; Linda Brooks; Michael Comerford; Patrick Dragonette; Simon Elliot; Wyndell Hamilton; Hillary Jones; Juergen Nogai; Carol Price; Barbara Sinatra; and Sonya Stewart.

Mark Davidson of Mark Davidson Photography brought his great eye to the project and provided the majority of the photographs in this book. The management, editorial, design, and production team at Vendome Press (Mark Magowan, Jim Spivey, and Celia Fuller) were critical to the process of producing a book of the highest quality.

I am thankful to Michael Smith who was so very generous in offering his personal views in the foreword. I am also thankful to Peter Schifando, who graciously allowed access to the archives of William Haines Designs and provided images of previously unpublished original material to enhance the book. My gratitude goes most of all to Stephen Drucker who brought his editorial and publishing expertise to the project and shaped a book that captures the best of the design vocabulary of Sunnylands and presents it in a compelling way.

Janice Lyle, PhD
Director, Sunnylands Center & Gardens

INDEX

Italic pages indicate illustrations.

PHOTOGRAPHY CREDITS

Front Cover: Mark Davidson, 2016. Back Cover: Derry Moore, 2002. Page 1: Mark Davidson, 2015. Pages 2–3, 4–5: Ken Hayden, 2014. Pages 6–7: Ken Hayden, 2012. Page 8: Mark Davidson, 2015. Pages 10–11: Ken Hayden, 2014. Page 12: Mark Davidson, 2016. Pages 14–15: Marc Glassman, 2016. Pages 16, 17: Graydon Wood, 2006. Pages 18, 19: Mark Davidson, 2015. Pages 21, 22: Sunnylands Collection. Page 23: ©2016. TV Guide. 123246:0416WH. Pages 24, 25: Gloria Etting, 1968. Page 26: Mark Davidson, 2012. Page 27: Sunnylands Collection. Page 28: Mark Davidson, 2015. Page 29: Sunnylands Collection. Pages 30–31: Sibylle Allgaier, 2012. Pages 32 (top), 33: Permission to reproduce: Hillary, Michael, and Timothy Jones. Page 32 (bottom): Sunnylands Collection. Pages 34–35, 36–37, 38–39: Sunnylands Collection. Pages 40–41: Drawing by and courtesy of Harry W. Saunders, AIA, 2007. Pages 42–43: © Sunnylands Photography J. Shulman & J. Nogai, 2007 ©Juergen Nogai. Page 44 (top left): Mark Davidson, 2016; (top right): Mark Davidson, 2016; (bottom): Ken Hayden, 2012. Page 45 (top): Mark Davidson, 2015; (bottom): Mark Davidson, 2016; (right): Ken Hayden, 2014. Pages 46, 47: Harry Saunders, Sunnylands Collection. Pages 48, 49: Sunnylands Collection. Pages 50–51, 52–53: All rights reserved. Peter Schifando and William Haines Designs. Pages 54, 55: Harry Saunders, Sunnylands Collection. Page 56: All rights reserved. Peter Schifando and William Haines Designs. Page 57: Mark Davidson, 2016. Pages 58, 59, 60, 61 (bottom): All rights reserved. Peter Schifando and William Haines Designs. Page 61 (top): Mark Davidson, 2015. Pages 62–63, 64–65: All rights reserved. Peter Schifando and William Haines Designs. Page 66: Mark Davidson, 2015. Pages 67, 68–69: All rights reserved. Peter Schifando and William Haines Designs. Pages 70, 71: Mark Davidson, 2015. Pages 72–73: Graydon Wood, 2006. Page 76: Mark Davidson, 2016. Page 77: Ken Hayden, 2012. Pages 78–79, 80–81: Mark Davidson, 2016. Pages 82, 83: Mark Davidson, 2012. Pages 84–85: Ken Hayden, 2012. Pages 86, 87, 88: Mark Davidson, 2015. Page 89: Ned Redway, 2008. Pages 90–91: Mark Davidson, 2015. Pages 92–93: Graydon Wood, 2006. Pages 94–95, 96, 97, 98: Mark Davidson, 2015. Page 99: David Glomb, 2010. Page 100: Graydon Wood, 2006. Page 101 (top): Jason Ware, 2015. Page 101 (bottom): Graydon Wood, 2006. Page 102: Mark Davidson, 2014. Pages 102–3: Graydon Wood, 2006. Page 104: Ken Hayden, 2012. Pages 106–7: Taili Song Roth, 2013. Pages 108–9, 110: Graydon Wood, 2006. Page 111 (top): Mark Davidson, 2012. Page 111 (right, bottom): David Glomb, 2010. Pages 112–13: Ken Hayden, 2012. Pages 114–15: White House Photo, December 31, 1988. Page 116: Mark Davidson, 2016. Page 117: Ken Hayden, 2012. Pages 118–19: Mark Davidson, 2016. Pages 120, 121: Mark Davidson, 2015. Pages 122–23: Ken Hayden, 2012. Pages 124, 125: Mark Davidson, 2016. Page 126: Mark Davidson, 2015. Pages 128–29: Mark Davidson, 2016. Pages 130–31, 132–33: Mark Davidson, 2015. Page 134 (top): Daniel Modlin, 2013. Page 134 (bottom): Ken Hayden, 2012. Page 135: Mark Davidson, 2015. Pages 136–37, 138–39: Mark Davidson, 2016. Pages 140–41: Ken Hayden, 2012. Pages 142, 143: Mark Davidson, 2015. Pages 144–45: Ken Hayden, 2012. Page 145 (top and bottom), 146, 147: Mark Davidson, 2015. Pages 148–49: Daniel Modlin, 2015. Page 150: Mark Davidson, 2016. Page 151 (top): Ken Hayden, 2012. Page 151 (bottom): Mark Davidson, 2015. Page 152 (top): Mark Davidson, 2015. Page 152 (bottom): Ken Hayden, 2015. Page 153: Mark Davidson, 2016. Pages 154–55: Mark Davidson, 2015. Page 157: Sibylle Allgaier, 2012. Page 159: Sunnylands Collection. Page 161: Sibylle Allgaier, 2012. Pages 162–63: Scott Avra, 2013. Pages 164, 165: Derry Moore, 2002. Pages 166–67: Marc Glassman, 2016. Pages 168–69: Ken Hayden, 2014. Pages 170–71, 172–73: Mark Davidson, 2015. Pages 174–75: Marion Brenner, 2015. Pages 176–77: Derry Moore, 2002. Pages 178–79: Sunnylands Collection. Pages 180–81: Daniel Modlin, 2015. Pages 182, 183: Gloria Etting, 1968. Page 184: Sunnylands Collection. Page 185: Mark Davidson, 2015. Page 186: Ken Hayden, 2012. Page 187: Daniel Modlin, 2015. Pages 188–89: Marc Glassman, 2015. Pages 190–91: Sibylle Allgaier, 2013. Page 193: White House Photo, December 31, 1981. Pages 194–95: Sunnylands Collection. Page 196: White House Photo, December 31, 1982. Page 199: Gloria Etting, 1968. Page 200: all Sunnylands Collection, except (bottom right): White House Photo, February 14, 1995; (top left): Marc Glassman, 2000. Page 201: Sunnylands Collection. Pages 202–3: White House Photo, January 1, 1983. Page 204: Sunnylands Collection. Page 205 (clockwise from top right): White House Photos, December 31, 1982, 1987, 1983, 1984, and 1986. Pages 206–7: White House Photo, December 31, 1985. Page 209: Sunnylands Collection. Page 210: Mark Davidson, 2011. Page 211: Sunnylands Collection. Pages 212–13: White House Photo, March 3,1990. Pages 214–15: White House Photo, March 3, 1990. Pages 216, 217, 218, 219: Sunnylands Collection. Pages 220, 221: David Sutton, 1976. Pages 222, 223: Sunnylands Collection. Pages 224, 225, 226–27: Gloria Etting, 1968. Pages 228–29: White House Photo, January 2, 1984. Page 231: Mark Davidson, 2011. Pages 232–33: Mark Davidson, 2014. Pages 234–35: White House Photo, June 2013. Pages 236–37: White House Photo, February 2016. Page 238 (clockwise from top): Mark Davidson, 2014; White House Photo, February 14, 2014; Mark Davidson, 2016; Mark Davidson, 2012; Mark Davidson, 2012. Page 239: Mark Davidson, 2014. Pages 240–41: Ken Hayden, 2014. Pages 242–43: Ken Haydon, 2012. Page 244: Mark Davidson, 2012. Page 245: Ken Hayden, 2014. Pages 246–47: Marion Brenner, 2015. Pages 248–49: White House Photo, June 8, 2013.

First published in the United States of America by
THE VENDOME PRESS
www.vendomepress.com

Library of Congress Control Number: 2016939094

ISBN 978-0-86565-331-3

Editor Stephen Drucker
Production Director Jim Spivey
Designer Celia Fuller

This book was produced using acid-free paper, processed chlorine free, and printed with soy-based inks.

Printed in China by OGI
First printing

Page 1 This ceramic emblem, created by William Haines Designs, was given as a memento to the Annenbergs before the project was finished in 1966.

Pages 2–3 The iconic, pink pyramidal roof captures the color of the mountains at sunrise and sunset.

Pages 4–5 The entrance fountain is a bronze column featuring symbols from Mexico's history. Created for the Annenbergs by José and Tomás Chávez Morado in 1968, it is a twenty-foot replica of the one at the Museo Nacional de Antropología in Mexico City.

Pages 6–7 "Upon first entering Sunnylands," says vintage Haines dealer Patrick Dragonette, "I was struck by the sheer volume of space and the magic that is the work of William Haines. His ability to take an immense room and have it feel intimate and personal was one of his great gifts. The fact that his furniture is both beautiful and ever so comfortable makes it all the better."

Page 8 Ceiling-height front doors open to numerous seating areas surrounding the atrium. Black marble borders were used to align the furniture. The brass door hardware is surprisingly florid for such a modern house.

Page 10 Architect A. Quincy Jones employed the egg crate–coffered ceiling as a major element both inside and outside the house. At the front entrance, it forms a cantilevered canopy.